JAMES LEWIS, JR.

A CONTEMPORARY
APPROACH TO
NONGRADED EDUCATION

Parker Publishing Company, Inc.

West Nyack, New York

To

Michael, Patricia, Terence

and

Valdmir, my wife

ACKNOWLEDGMENTS

This book is the result of two years of extensive travel throughout the United States, visiting nongraded schools in action, and spending countless hours conferring with noted educators, including Dr. Robert A. Anderson at Harvard University, Dr. Maurie Hilson at Rutgers University; Dr. Martha Dawson at Hampton Institute; Dr. Charles Raebeck at Dowling College; Drs. Theodore McFadden and John Carr Duff, of Hofstra University; Dr. George Thomas of the New York State Education Department; and Dr. Leonard Schwartz, Director of the Institute for Sensitivity Training for Educational Programming. Considerable material for this book also resulted from the author's attendance at numerous workshops and conferences on the nongraded concept and sensitivity training, buttressed by voluminous research into a multitude of books and articles pertaining to the nongraded philosophy, as well as extensive written correspondence with more than 400 nongraded schools scattered throughout the nation.

The author is deeply indebted to all of the foregoing, as well as to the staff members of the Wyandanch School District and students and parents in the Wyandanch community for their contributions of materials, suggestions, and advice without which this book could not have been written. The author acknowledges a special debt to Mr. James Butler, Principal of the Milton L. Olive Elementary School in Wyandanch, Long Island, New York for his critical and painstaking review of the final manuscript.

No less large a measure of gratitude does the author feel toward his special assistant, Y'vonne Carrington, and the three blessed secretaries, Gloria Roman, Rita Brown, and Ellen Gove who patiently, and with heavenly forbearance, applied their excellent skills through a multitude of drafts to the production of a final manuscript.

I shall pass through this world but once. Any good therefore that I can do or any kindness that I can show to any human being, let me do it now. Let me not defer or neglect it for I shall not pass this way again.

FOREWORD

Kenneth Boulding has said, "If the human race is to survive it will have to change its ways of thinking more in the next 25 years than in the last 25,000." Similarly, the weekly journal MANAS in a recent issue stated that "The formulation of what education is or ought to be is undergoing radical alteration. From being a question of how to transmit to the young our accumulated knowledge, it is turning into a question of how to change the characteristic patterns of human behavior."

It is no longer necessary to make a case for the immediate need for broadly conceived programs of educational reform. Wherever the fortuitous combination of educational concern plus the potential for creative response exists, reform is inevitable. Within the educational establishment such spearheads of reform are multiplying daily.

Unlike the educational scene of a few scant years ago, today we in education have become, whether we wish it or not, part of a revolutionary awakening. Call it "sensitivity training," "innovation," the "multi-university," "headstart," "upward bound," "the ungraded school," "student revolt," "teacher militancy," "decentralization," "relevance," "electronic education," "team teaching," etc., the unavoidable condition of professional life for the contemporary educator-teacher is one of continuous and radical reform.

Our first graders will have reached one of the significant phases of human maturity at the turn of the century when they approach 40 years of age. In my judgment, their ability to survive and to enjoy life will rest primarily upon the quality of their interpersonal relationships or, to put it another way, their ability to enter into the "human community."

In this book, Mr. Lewis gives fresh impetus not only to the pressing need for educational reform, but to reform within a context of humanization.

Mr. Lewis' contemporary approach to nongraded education strikes at the major stumbling block to the ideal of equal educational opportunity, namely, the present system of standardized curriculum and teaching practices with its parasitic host of ego-debilitating grading and marking procedures. He does this, not only as a man of theory, but as a practicing Chief School Administrator, by clarifying and applying to his beliefs the educational ethic of humanization and a valid form for its expression — the nongraded school.

For those who choose to "be involved" in the never ending quest for greater humanization of the educational environment, Mr. Lewis' work should provide much needed encouragement, insight and direction.

DR. CHARLES RAEBECK
Director of Teacher Education
Dowling College
Oakdale, New York

Schools must be organized so that each individual student, with unique capabilities, interests, and background can develop the full measure of his talent.

Donald C. Manlove

A WORD FROM THE AUTHOR
ABOUT THIS BOOK....

This book was written because of my belief that there exists a compelling need to better understand nongraded education. Undoubtedly, the book will mean different things to different educators. To some educators it may serve as an awakening; to other educators it will serve as a handy guide; and to still others, it will serve as a warning.

Today, the American public school system has made great strides in making a quantity of schools available to its youth; however, there is a great need for improvement in the quality of American public school education programs. Many educators are faced with the realization that the methods being used are not accomplishing the task of providing equally effective educational opportunity to all children. Obviously, there must be an immediate and radical change.

Ironically, the recent focus on the problems of the culturally "different" child not only served to increase our awareness of the many deficiencies in the educational programs we offer him, but also aroused the suspicion that the present educational system is not really answering the needs of an even larger number of American children. It is an appalling fact that there is a 50-50 chance that the culturally different child will not graduate from secondary school. Out of 50 children, only an approximate 25 will enter institutions of higher learning. Of those 25, only eight to ten young men and women have the educational advantages conferred by successful completion of undergraduate work. Since the culturally different child is quite often a victim of poverty, and if we accept the estimate of leading sociologists that there are approximately 32,000,000 Americans who would be characterized as low-income population, the future ramifications of present educational deficiencies on the American society with its present high reproductive rates cannot be minimized. Already some of the consequences of our failure to subvert the educational lag are evident in the unrest among college students, incidences of cheating on examinations, boycotts, student strikes, and in the high incidence of school dropouts or "stay-ins" who find school irrelevant and simply absorb enough material to pass tests.

Among these consequences, which have been well-documented by statistics, are the poor self images acquired by some students due to punishment "techniques" of holding back or failing those students who do not absorb the required amount of material, and the pressures on and ostracism of certain students which lead them to become disruptive students in order to gain the individualized attention they seek. An equally disturbing result of the inefficacies of the present educational system is the aversion felt by a number of gifted, potential teachers toward entering a field which seems to be an empire built on mediocrity, primarily intent on maintenance of the status quo, which evidences a high incidence of instability or "turnover" among its members, particularly those assigned to areas designated as "hard-core."

With something akin to panic, a number of short-term, unrealistic measures have been foisted upon the public as designs which will have a salubrious effect. A great deal of emphasis has been placed on remediation via the avenues of compensatory education and desegregation, as approaches which will solve the ills of our present-day school system. However, as is true of our society, and even more true in the field of education, we need to seek a more humanistic approach; i.e., to accomplish a humanistic transformation in all of our interactions with other human beings, be they mature or immature. The nongraded philosophy prescribes the ideal manner in which the transition from traditionalism to humanism may be effected. Where the individual child is of prime value and represents the focal point of the entire educational program, he receives that element which is usually absent from his educational life – an obvious manifestation of the "I care" attitude.

Although there are over 2,000 schools in the country which are represented as "nongraded" these schools have not implemented what really constitutes an accurate version of the nongraded concept.

Why are there so few genuine nongraded schools or programs? Why are educators reluctant to make the necessary changes? Why do educators persist in deceiving themselves, either constructively or destructively, insofar as nongraded vs. traditional education is concerned? There are several possible answers to these simple queries. Generally, educators will continue to seek new ideas if they feel the ideas will improve the education of children. To arrive at this certainty, educators will usually look for the following three elements they consider basic:

1. The idea is not revolutionary in nature;
2. The idea does not tend to upset what they regard as the balance of the status quo; and
3. The idea contains small risk of failure.

In other words, some educators tend to be cautious people. This is, perhaps, an occupational hazard carried down from the early days of public education when the life of an educator was severely restricted by social mores. Actually, most present-day educators are aware that they are not reaching as many classroom students as they would like to. Therefore, some of them are eager to attempt new ideas which they take up for their novelty, but then inculcate in practice with the three elements of caution mentioned above, proudly maintaining that "our schools are nongraded in nature." Part of this, no doubt, is due to the thought expressed by Dr. Robert H. Anderson to the effect that everyone likes to get in on a good thing, and in this lies the reason for a plethora of false claims to nongradedness.

The most important questions, however, are: Where do we go from here? How do we really nongrade schools? The initial step must, of necessity, consist of thoroughly re-educating educators so that they accept, without reservations, the contention that the job of educating students in public schools is not being done properly and that constructive steps are long overdue. This author does not prescribe change just for the sake of change, but rather changes for the improvement of education. In this context, he is reminded of two incidents which clearly indicate the general reluctance on the part of many educators to make constructive changes. The first incident occurred at a Parent-Teacher Association meeting in a local high school, where a well-known professor from one of the nearby colleges delivered an address on the merits of nongraded education. Several principals from surrounding school districts who were in attendance at the meeting became visibly upset over what they considered to be a denunciation of public school education. The professor was, in fact, simply suggesting ways of making the educational process more effective for students. The principals, however, becoming increasingly incensed, refused to listen and stormed out of the auditorium en masse. The second incident also involved a well-known professor, this time from Stanford University, who addressed a group of educators attending a sensitivity training workshop. The professor commented on the dynamics of change, humanizing education, the evils of traditional education, and the need for administrators to willingly undertake changes. One superintendent present became so annoyed that he rose to his feet after the address and with a livid face and loud voice castigated the professor, shouting: "You don't know what you are talking about; you live in an ivory tower. You are a disgrace to education."

These incidents illustrate the fact that traditional education can become so deeply embedded in the minds of some educators that it presents a formidable obstacle to any examination of what we are actually accomplishing and what we hope to accomplish in education, wherein lies the most direct path to success. Certainly, knowledge of test scores and of the numerous publications dealing with case histories of children who are not being properly educated, indicates that educators should be more than willing to attempt to improve education in the public schools.

Just a glance at the attrition rate in completion of formal education gives ample food for thought. By comparison, a nongraded philosophy which emphasizes the individual worth of students — which includes and promotes education that is public relations oriented in demanding that educators be able to relate to students as human beings in order to "sell" education to them — appears to be the only sound, humane, and logical way of imparting knowledge.

CONTENTS

15

of the Graph Method. Advantages and Disadvantages of the Chart Method. Graded Report Card vs. Nongraded Report Card. Cumulative Records. Conference Method. Advantages and Disadvantages of Conference Method. Periodic Pupil Progress Report. Suggested Practices When Planning the Nongraded Report Card. Teacher Training and Reporting Pupil Progress. Explaining the Nongraded Report Card to Parents.

Achievement Testing. Student and Parent Attitude Scale. Teacher Attitude Scale. Student Reaction Assessment. Nongraded Consultants or Experts. The Nongraded Checklist.

Preparing Today for Tomorrow's Changes. The Role of Parents. The Role of Educational Professionals. The Role of Higher Institutions. The Role of Students. The Role of State Education Officials. Future Developments.

APPENDICES

1. DEFINING THE

NONGRADED CONCEPT

The nongraded school is based on the principle that not all students learn all things equally well or with equal speed. Neither are all equally interested in education nor does everyone care to pursue it to the same degree.

B. Frank Brown

In a relatively short span of time, the nongraded concept has made a profound impression on thousands of elementary schools throughout the country. However, as might be expected with any broad and innovative program, there tends to be a great deal of misunderstanding leading to misrepresentation of schools as "nongraded" which do not fully embrace the true nongraded philosophy. Most of the nongraded schools observed by the author on his tour simply provided the kind of organization that flowed around a system of homogeneous grouping. There were also some schools which used the Joplin Plan to a lesser or greater degree. Neither homogeneous grouping nor the Joplin Plan are ideal for fostering individualization of instruction. For example, many school administrators interpreted the nongraded concept as being synonymous with homogeneous grouping, while a professor of a local college emphatically stated to a group of students that nongrading was ability grouping. One young teacher being interviewed for a position indicated that the nongraded concept was a form of team teaching.

The obvious fact is that none of these professional educators knew what the correct definition of the nongraded concept encompassed. It may be that their opinions were influenced by the thousands of schools throughout the country which have implemented their own versions of a nongraded program. In actuality, schools which have successfully implemented the true nongraded concept are distressingly few in number.

A fault may lie with the failure of our universities to adequately present the nongraded concept, the absence of a model nongraded school, and/or the reluctance of administrators to make changes. For instance, many university professors advocate the nongraded philosophy but conduct lectures and seminars which are severely limited in scope, because too few professors have actually experienced the realities of implementing or working in a nongraded environment. In any event, and whatever the cause for the current misunderstanding, it is essential that a true definition of the nongraded philosophy be expounded.

The Individualization of Instruction

In order to explain the nongraded concept best, it will perhaps be useful to first enumerate the things which it is not. It is not heterogeneous grouping where children are assigned to a class without regard for age, ability, or other relevant factors. It is not homogeneous grouping where children are assigned according to ability or some other common denominator. It is not team teaching which utilizes those particularly outstanding assets of a teacher to produce a more flexible educational program. It is not flexible scheduling where students are assigned to modules of varied length according to their interest in and the requirements of a particular subject area. It is not computer-assisted instruction where pupils may receive instructions from a computer which has programmed lessons. It is not individually prescribed instruction where teachers prescribe instructions for particular students. It is not educational technology where various educative machines, television, and audio-visual materials aid the teacher in the instructional process.

However, many of these instructional procedures can and should be a part of any effective nongraded program. In other words, we must think of the nongraded concept as a whole which is equal to the sum of all its parts.

The basic guiding principle behind the nongraded concept is individualization of instruction. Any efficacious ways and means adopted by educators to individualize instruction serves to foster the goals of the nongraded philosophy. The nongraded concept must embrace attempts to meet the social, educational, emotional, and physical needs of all children by the proper utilization of a flexible program, employing a variety of methods, materials, and equipment in the educational process.

The nongraded philosophy permits greater socialization among students, providing an atmosphere where they may talk about common interests and mutual problems, arriving at decisions based on logic, discussion, and a democratic exchange procedure. It also provides an opportunity for the implementation of an educational program geared to the individual child's interests, needs, and values.

A more healthy emotional climate for learning is provided by the nongraded educational philosophy which permits a child to learn at his own rate of speed, according to his own capabilities, and without fearing the ogre of failure or the humiliation of not being able to achieve equally with another student. An improved self-image, giving the child a sense of his own worth and value with which he can be happy, does much to enhance his exuberance and enjoyment at each stage of his development.

Humanism, a Basic Ingredient

A program which provides for individualization of instruction is not truly a nongraded program, unless humanism is an integral part of the program. What is humanism? In education, it means seeing and treating students as individuals, each with a different personality, needs, interests, and abilities. It means recognizing the common humanity of all people. It means that children in a classroom go home with a feeling of success each day. It means an educational process in which human beings, the teachers and students, learn from each other. It means a school atmosphere which is warm and supportive so that students feel wanted, respected, and liked. It means acceptance and caring about students' human qualities. In essence, humanism in education means being a teacher who is sensitively alive.

A true illustration of the results of humanism in the classroom has been conveyed to the author by a close friend who is presently teaching in a deprived area in Newark, New Jersey. This teacher explained that only three of his 29 students were living with their natural fathers. He then related the story of one child whose father had died recently. When, immediately following the funeral services, the mother was quite naturally overcome with emotion and crying, the student placed his arms around his mother saying: "Don't cry, I have another father in school." Obviously, this teacher well knew the ingredients of humanism in a classroom, for there are times when a teacher who is sensitively alive must play the role of both mother and father to his students.

At one time, the author was scheduled to deliver a speech to members of his faculty on the opening day of school on the topic of "Humanism in Education." Although the speech had been prepared in advance for him to read from, as he stood up and faced the audience the realization suddenly struck him with great force and clarity that, after all, the most humanistic way in which to explain humanism was not to read from a cold, previously prepared speech, but to observe the reactions and try to feel the needs of the audience in front of him as he pursued his topic. From the comments which followed his delivery, it was obvious that the extemporaneous speech was much more effective than the stale, prepared one would have been. There follows a transcription from that speech as it was recorded:

> Good Morning. I welcome all of you, both new and old staff members, who will begin what I believe will be a highly successful school year of advancement for Wyandanch students. I refer, of course, to the efforts we will make to humanize education at Wyandanch so that it becomes a personal exploration and experience for both the educator and the student. As you are all aware, we are intensely concerned with meeting the needs of all Wyandanch students. However, in order to do this effectively, we as educators, are faced with the task of questioning ourselves with regard to the ever changing world in which we live; our hopes and goals in our profession; and our own needs as humans. In other words, a teacher is not simply a perambulating vessel of facts which can be tilted to let so much out and keep so much in. Nor is a student simply an empty receptacle which passively accepts these facts. Because we live in a highly technological and changing environment, many of these facts will be outdated by the time our students seek to use them. Our goal then, must be to facilitate the learning process, constantly nurturing the inquiring spirit so that learning and change are interrelated.

Knowledge alone cannot, in our modern world, serve as a base of continuing security. Security rests on the process of seeking knowledge, of learning how to learn, and how to adopt and change, with a reliance on process rather than upon static knowledge.

It is unfortunate that our increasing emphasis on mechanization has spilled over onto the personal relationship between the student and teacher, which is the most basic element in the facilitation of learning. Dehumanization in the educative process serves only to thwart the goals of both student and teacher while, at the same time, transforming future societies into intellectual cripples.

Facilitating the learning process is a very personal experience for both teacher and student. The teacher and students must interact first as human beings, involved with each other, caring about each other, respecting and trusting each other before any seeking and giving may take place, before any thirsty inquiry may be given creative response, and before any significant, self-initiated learning by the whole person can be achieved. We, as educators at Wyandanch, will use our teaching skills; we will use all of our scholarly knowledge; we will carefully plan curriculum; we will use textbooks and we will make presentations — all of these are important resources. But, the most important resource is ourselves and we will facilitate learning by the attitudinal qualities which we bring into existence in our personal relationship with Wyandanch students. We must strive to cast aside the facades and veneers and bring reality into the learning process by creating a human atmosphere which stimulates free curiosity and the necessary excitement which transforms all students into a community of learners.

This can only be done if we continually make an effort to know ourselves, to know our students, and bearing this knowledge in mind, to humanize the educational process so that it serves these human beings existing in the world as we know it. We can no longer depend on half-truths; we must accept the challenge of uncovering the whole truth as it applies to ourselves and our students. We speak of a curriculum which "covers" certain areas. We must be certain that the dual definitions of "cover" — "to take in" and "to conceal from view" — do not intrude falsity into our educational atmosphere. We are all aware of the distortions in courses "covering" American History which heap praise upon the Abraham Lincolns and cast the John Browns in villainous roles; which do not question the propriety of taking land from "savage" Indians or enslaving "primitive" Africans, although preaching the principles of democracy and brotherly love in an educational facility from which the American flag proudly waves alone, effectively denying the symbolism which a flag of the United Nations would inspire. To the seekers after knowledge who come into Wyandanch classrooms, we must offer whole truths in and of ourselves, basing the learning process on the importance of the students as individuals, and destroying the forces of alienation and depersonalization. In this context, we cannot be successful unless we involve ourselves with the truths of our own attitudes, the truths of the students' inner reactions, and the truths inherent in the knowledge we seek to convey. "To be human is to err." Many mistakes have been made in the past and, most probably, many mistakes will be made in the future. Man automatically learns from his mistakes; we do not have to concentrate on them. We do have to concentrate on being humane and sensitive. Our task then, is to facilitate learning, to build the curriculum and the school district around the needs of the students as we are able to interpret them from our own personal interaction and involvement with the student. A student who is thus made an integral participant in the learning process will grow with the curriculum and the school district — he will be eager to learn — he will not be forced to become a dropout, nor will he be forced to resort to disruptive actions to prove that he is that most valuable commodity — an individual human being.

Although it is easy to espouse the concept of performing as a human being in the classroom it seems much more difficult to put the concept into practice. This may, of course, be a national problem which has permeated the classroom. Each day, we are apprised of instances of inhumanity and cruelty in our world such as those occurring in Biafra and Vietnam. How does one react to a world which seems to be the "oyster" of inhuman creatures who think only of themselves and never of the consequences they impose on other human beings? How do we get those people who do have a humane concern and sensitivity to the needs of others to refrain from smothering these tendencies? How do we eliminate the label of "sucker" which is too often applied to those who readily exhibit humanism toward their fellowmen? How can we change the world we live in into a place of peaceful coexistence, and how can we transform the classroom atmosphere into a humane educational setting when we have been practicing inhumanity in the classroom since 1848? These questions are profound and there are many possible answers which have some merits. They must all be considered in light of the possibility that, perhaps, many inhumane incidents occur simply because we take humanism so much "for granted." We can no longer passively "suppose" that humanism exists in the classroom, but must seek its existence and carefully nurture its growth. If humanism is to begin anywhere, and if we acknowledge the importance of hydra-like manifestations of humanism, then a classroom of children must be the home of humanism if there is to be any hope for future men.

Humanistic Demand for the Nongraded Concept

For centuries, parents have been aware that no two children are alike. Great philosophers too, like Kant in the eighteenth century, stressed that the only true education would be one that concentrated on the development of an individual's natural gifts which would make the full man. Plato stressed that:

> Knowledge which is acquired under compulsion has no hold on the mind. Therefore, do not use compulsion, but let early education be rather a sort of amusement, this will better enable you to find out the natural bent of the child.[1]

Finally, educators now admit that their previous attempts to confine each child to the absorption of a crusty mold of ritualized information within a specified time may have left a great deal to be desired. It is difficult to understand and, indeed, sadly ironic that parents did not, in the past, rise up in arms against school authorities for adhering to the concept that at a given age all children can be expected to have the same capabilities and benefit from the same kind of instruction.

Philosophy, as defined in Webster's Dictionary[2], is the "pursuit of wisdom, search for truth through logical reasoning rather than factual observation." In just this fashion does the nongraded concept seek to educate the child to actively pursue wisdom rather than

---

[1] Will Durant, "The Republic, Plato," *Story of Philosophy* (New York: Simon & Schuster, Inc., 1933), p. 34.

[2] *Webster's Seventh New Collegiate Dictionary* (Springfield, Mass: G. & C. Merriam Co., 1967), p. 635.

sitting passively and have the words of wisdom of an instructor din upon his ears. We are mindful of Socrates' view that a teacher is only a midwife to his pupil's thoughts. We would have the student, through the medium of individualized instruction, receive information pertinent to the queries fostered by his interest level – then we would have him question further and pursue his search for truth by utilizing the expertise of team teacher specialists and through independent study at adequate informational material centers. We would, in other words, encourage his own logical reasoning. The nongraded philosophy calls for "the workshop, the laboratory, the materials and the tools with which the child may construct, create and actively inquire, and even the requisite space combined in an atmosphere . . . where activity on the part of the children preceded the giving of information on the part of the teacher, or where the children had some motive for demanding the information,"[3] as envisioned by John Dewey.

The nongraded philosophy is completely rational in its approach, which takes into account the vastness and variety of the tasks in which the individuals we are educating today will be involved in the future. We must prepare them, as best we can, for whatever may come in the twenty-first century. Traditional education will not suffice, even as it does not today. When ours was primarily an agricultural society, small doses of knowledge were sufficient for the masses. We cannot afford this irrational waste of the potentials of millions of citizens in what we can presuppose will be a highly technological age demanding high levels of skills, ability, and interest. Education must take the lead in providing our masses with large and varied doses of the medicine of knowledge. While, of course, a wee child is much unlike a horse, the analogy serves perfectly to describe our educational system which has been leading our students to the doors of knowledge and deserting them. We must make them drink long and deeply, and this author firmly believes that individualized instruction offered in the nongraded curriculum is the only way of accomplishing this.

In recent years, psychologists have used empirical evidence to support their theories of the individuality of each mite of humanity.

---

[3] John Dewey, *The School and Society* (University of Chicago Press, 1956), p. 32.

This theory has been clearly elucidated by Russ Stagner and T. F. Korwoski in the following summary:

> All organisms are capable of learning, but some learn faster than others; some achieve a higher level of complexity than others; some are especially adept at one type of material, but not at others. In every psychological function, individual humans differ from each other in many ways . . . [4]

The nongraded concept maintains that children are not alike and each child should be educated differently. It is the whole individual child shaped by his heredity, his maturation, his environmental experiences, and his own special, unique abilities and personality that we must focus upon in order to make any instructional program successful. Noted psychologists, in stressing that successful educational practices rest on more than maturational readiness alone, call attention to the structuring of the material to be learned in suitable form for the learner, the arousal of appropriate motives, and the acquisition of necessary prior learning.

Obviously, the theory that all children of a given age must submit to exposure to and the absorption of a given amount of material in specific areas fails to take into consideration any other aspect of the individual except maturational or age readiness. If we know that children grasp their bottles, crawl, walk, climb, babble, and speak at different ages, why do we not likewise accept the logical conclusion that each child will also grasp varied information in the learning process at different ages? Why do we excite humiliation or envy in a child by forcing him to compare his own worth with the worth of others in the age-locked classroom when he really should compare himself with a concept of his own reason? Should we not also, as sensitive adults engrossed in the chores of educating the next generation, remove the instruments whereby one child may humiliate another? Are we being compassionate and concerned with the needs of each child when we punish a few by failure because they do not absorb what we in our pristine podiums have decreed to be a necessary maximum of content at a certain age?

---

[4] Russ Stagner and T. F. Korwoski, *Psychology* (New York: McGraw-Hill Book Company, Inc., 1952), p. 23.

The Educational Appropriateness of the Nongraded Concept

Individualized instruction which permits each child to progress at his own level of interest and ability lies at the core of the nongraded concept. Rather than stretch and fit the child into the groove of the instruction, it proposes to stretch and fit the instruction to the individual child. Interest level is obviously important in view of the innate differences in individuals which give our civilization gifted men of such widely varied pursuits as an Einstein and a Walt Whitman; a builder of bridges and a doctor of medicine; or an inventor of the atom bomb and a painter of pictures. The list could be unending — just as are the individual differences in interest level of each child. And yet, in our public education system, we would have made an Einstein and a Whitman conform to the same mold. Making the child the focal point of individualized instruction in our schools according to his interest level and ability will obviously be more effective than the Procrustean method — most especially so, as applied to the culturally different child in our society who attends one of the many ghetto schools in low-income neighborhoods all over the United States. Indeed, it would seem that this type of individualized instruction would provide an effective weapon against continuing educational deficiencies, with the attendant waste of human resources, which beset a large segment of our society. More than any other person, perhaps, the culturally different child needs to be treated as an individual in an effective educational system, rather than as part of a group which is expected to learn 100 percent of content which is being relentlessly poured out by a withdrawn lecturer. The author believes in the more productive, humanistic approach to education that is manifested in a personalized relationship which is the initial beginning of the nongraded concept. The individual child is the entire focal point of the instructional program at all times.

The Role of the Principal in a Nongraded School

The principal is the chief administrator and supervisor of the building. The major responsibility of arousing and maintaining teacher interest in the nongraded concept lies with him. He will also have to arrange schedules which make allowances for teacher visitation to other nongraded schools. He should be adept at or acquire the facility for writing proposals for financing to help subsidize certain aspects of the nongraded program. Since he will be the prime resource person, he must possess or acquire a wide range of knowledge pertaining to the nongraded concept. It is essential that he be versatile in training and approach so that, on occasion, he can assume the following roles:

1. The role of a coordinator who is able to get the teaching staff to function together as a team so that each member may make his maximum contribution to the nongraded program.

2. The role of an instigator who can provide the necessary impetus to get the staff involved completely in the nongraded program.

3. The role of an educational engineer who is able to organize and structure the nongraded program in order to provide maximum opportunities for individualization of instruction.

4. The role of a research virtuoso who can bring together materials, resource persons, teachers, and students in a positive relationship so as to effectuate intellectual development and social growth in the nongraded program.

5. The role of an overseer who can develop and maintain the nongraded program which is written within the framework established by the Board of Education and the chief school administrator.

6. The role of an intellectual leader who makes contributions to the education of all students through the leadership which he provides to teachers attempting to develop special programs for particular needs and to implement those program facets into the curriculum.

7. The role of a diplomat who is able to relate effectively to the community so that he may keep them informed and continually abreast of the nongraded program's developments.

8. The role of a psychologist who is able to gain the necessary insights for making the most effective use of creative minds on his staff in order to bring additional advantages to the program.

The Role of the Teacher in the Nongraded Classroom

The nongraded teacher is no longer a lecturer who stands in front of the classroom preaching the gospel of the textbook at her students.* She must be the prime catalyst in the attempt to individualize the educational process so that students become interested in learning for learning's sake and remain eager to learn. It is necessary for her to present material in a variety of ways so that when a child fails to master material presented in one way, she can guide him to another method in which he may gain mastery. It is essential that she be sensitive to the needs of each individual child in her class through her humaneness and dedication to her profession. She must possess a wide range of talents which will enable her, on occasion, to assume:

1. The role of a motivator who can give the students inspiration to learn.

2. The role of a resource person who is capable of choosing just the right materials for the needs of a particular child.

3. The role of a social worker who takes an interest in the socialization aspects of a student's home life which affect his activities in the educational program.

4. The role of a psychologist and guidance counselor who delves under the surface to cope with hidden problems which act as a deterrent to learning unless ingenuity is used in providing evocative materials to overcome apathy.

5. The role of a diagnostician who, on occasion, can be as intuitive as a parent in determining what's wrong.

6. The role of a facilitator of learning who makes learning enjoyable to the learner because of the humane way in which material is presented.

The teacher who plays these roles well in the nongraded environment influences students so that they become the eager seekers after and recipients of the knowledge to which she can lead them.

The Role of the Student in the Nongraded Classroom

In the nongraded classroom, the student is responsible for much of his learning. This is not to lessen the role of the nongraded teacher

---

*Because of language limitations the feminine gender is used only for convenience, and the remarks which follow are, of course, equally applicable to all instructors, whether male or female.

as illustrated above, but to put the emphasis where it should have been in the first place — on the individual, rather than the mass. To do this, the teacher must be available to go to the aid of each and every student who has become perplexed over some subject matter.

1. The student must realize that he and his teacher will reach a personal relationship in the classroom that was absent in the traditionally oriented classroom, but is an essential feature of the nongraded classroom.

2. The student will begin to realize that, like himself, the teacher is also a human being with human capabilities and human limitations. It is important that the student realize that he will be an active participant in deciding how and what he will learn.

3. The student must be able to decide what materials best fit his own individual needs, interests, and abilities.

4. The student must be able to use effectively the multitude of educational technology that is available for his use in the classroom.

5. The student and parent will play a more vital role in deciding what education will be pursued in school, at home, and in other agencies.

6. The student must be able to work independently and do research by himself where called for.

7. The student must learn how to learn, so that he can get as much from his basic education as possible.

SUMMARY

The nongraded technique must include processes which humanize education and relate the educational program to the interests, abilities, and values of the individual child. It must involve the transition from traditionalism to humanism in reaching and educating all children, each in his own way. Humanism, an essential part of any nongraded program, must be fostered by principal, teacher, and student at all times. THE NONGRADED CONCEPT STRESSES INDIVIDUALIZATION OF INSTRUCTION IN THE MOST HIGHLY REFINED MANNER POSSIBLE.

The philosophical and psychological appropriateness of the nongraded techniques cannot be questioned. That many of the techniques which now form the theoretical basis for nongraded practices were suggested centuries ago constitutes almost a mockery of the advances modern man has made in other areas of inquiry, such as science and technology. However, it is never too late to rectify obvious errors in practice or techniques, once they are exposed to the logic of reasonable minds willing to undertake constructive change. Indeed, this is just what those educators who have taken their first, sometimes faltering, steps down the nongraded road are attempting to do.

2. PITFALLS TO AVOID
WHEN NONGRADING

In this case, the child becomes the ——————
—————— *sum about which the appliances of*
education revolve: he is the center
about which they are organized.

John Dewey

For too many centuries, the reverse of this philosopher's theory has been true, and each child has had to accommodate his revolutions to a system of education geared for all students rather than for each student. The modern approach, exemplified by the nongraded concept, decries the old passive education which mechanically meshed children through a uniform sieve of method and curriculum. What we refer to here as the "nongraded concept" has variously been expressed in other terms such as "ungraded concept," "continuous progress program," "continuous growth," "levels of achievement program," "achievement program," "achievement level grouping," and the "dual progress plan."

Professor Robert H. Anderson, one of the pioneers in implementing the concept of nongradedness, calls attention in his most recent volume to the fact that the slow acceptance and institution of the nongraded concept probably stems from the deficiencies inherent in the majority of such pilot programs.[1] He

---

[1] Robert A. Anderson, *Teaching in a World of Change* (New York: Harcourt Brace & Co., 1966), p. 51.

goes on to classify most of the efforts at nongrading between 1942 and the mid-1960's as falling into the following categories:

1. Serious efforts to give the idea full-scale development in a well-conceived form;
2. Serious efforts to implement one or more aspects of the nongraded idea in a well-conceived form;
3. Modest efforts to achieve nongrading within an inadequate theoretical frame of reference; and
4. Fraudulent or naive use of the vocabulary of nongradedness to describe what is in fact a conventional graded program.

This author agrees wholeheartedly with Professor Anderson's statements. A point deserving consideration lies in the failure of hundreds of nongraded schools in the country to implement in their programs desired objectives which are effective techniques to nongraded education. Unless teachers and administrators are aware of what constitutes a paragon to serve as a model for the effective nongraded school, even more schools will continue to make the mistakes and errors exhibited by the pseudo-nongraded schools now in existence. During the author's travels, he visited several outstanding nongraded schools throughout the country and noted both desirable features to be emulated and undesirable features to be shunned. The following elements should be carefully studied by schools wishing to evaluate their own nongraded program by equating the desirable and undesirable features which are incorporated in other nongraded systems.

Inappropriate Terminology

The use of terms such as "average," "slow," or "fast," in designating children or groups of children, must be abandoned completely. Such terminology reveals a regression to the old traditional, false conception that there exists such a creature as an "average" child when, in actuality, each "average" child differs immensely according to the judge and the yardstick used as a measure to reach judgment. The true nongraded concept, relying on the theory that each child has different interest levels, recognizes only achievement and mastery at different levels, in different areas, by different children within differentiated time spans.

Classification of Students

The popular use of the Intelligence Quotient (IQ) scale has a very limited place in a nongraded program. This device, based on a skewed curve, is and has been in nationwide use to determine the extent to which a child is capable of learning. For years, teachers have relied on the IQ device to judge and, sometimes, to classify students as "slow," "normal," "bright" or "gifted." A teacher committed to the nongraded philosophy must accept the basic principle that these terms can have no validity in a concept which eschews comparison of one child to another. The only valid standard of comparison to be applied is that of comparing the child's individual progress, i.e., a self-comparison at different stages of achievement. One of the more damaging aspects of teacher dependency on IQ classifications has been reported by Robert Rosenthal and Lenore Jacobson, in a study which includes the results of extensive research designed to measure the effects of teacher expectation on the intellectual growth of students. Teachers tend to rely heavily on standardized tests of intelligence and achievement in forming expectancy attitudes about an individual student. Unfortunately, these attitudes frequently restrict a student's activity to no more or less than the teacher expects of him. The Rosenthal study proved that when randomly selected students were assigned as subjects of a special test which demonstrated their potentials for significant intellectual growth, the resultant teacher expectancy played an important role in the actual achievement of the students who internalized teacher expectations and made significant gains. Rosenthal summarizes his study with the words:

> "On the basis of other experiments on interpersonal self-fulfilling prophecies, we can only speculate as to how teachers brought about intellectual competence simply by expecting it. Teachers may have treated their children in a more pleasant, friendly, and encouraging fashion when they expected greater intellectual gains of them. Such behavior has been shown to improve intellectual performance, probably by

its favorable effect on pupil motivation . . . There was only the belief that the children bore watching, that they had intellectual competencies that would in due course be revealed."[2]

It must be recognized that the results emerging from the study did not evolve as a result of crash reading programs, special tutoring or extra field trips.

The foregoing facts require that individual teachers in a nongraded program unequivocally discount Intelligence Quotient scores as measurements of potential. However, it is important to remember that the I.Q. can be of value to some extent in the educational program. For purposes of evaluation of the total nongraded program, it can be of inestimable value to administrators. For example, if an effective nongraded program is being implemented in a culturally different community, there is a great likelihood that, if measured before and after implementation of the nongraded program, the I.Q. level of the school will show an increase. However, such increase would not be as readily apparent in the more affluent school district. The foregoing assumption presupposes that the needs of culturally different students are not being met in the traditional educational program and, if their needs are not being met, they are not profiting from the educational program. Generally, these students become a discipline problem which constitutes a major area of concentration in most of the culturally different schools throughout the nation; or the school is burdened with high absentee and dropout rates which can be translated to the conclusion that students are not meeting with success in their school experience. In contrast, there is evidence that culturally different children in an effective nongraded environment attend school more regularly, provide fewer discipline problems, and achieve more out of their educational experiences in the individualized, nongraded program.

Usually, in a culturally different community, the median I.Q. score is somewhat lower than the average I.Q. in an affluent community. In addition to this, there is a standard deviation of approximately twenty-one points on the Binet-Wisc scales. Further disadvantages are inherent in the fact that, as a rule, the "middle

---

[2] Robert Rosenthal and Lenore Jacobson, *Pygmalion in the Classroom* (New York: Holt, Rinehart & Winston, Inc., 1968), pp. 180-181.

class" teacher tends to come into a classroom of "lower class" children equipped with a prejudgment of low expectancy, and this expectancy is even more particularly directed at male Negro students. As a result, teachers tend to hamper potential progress on the part of students because they are influenced by preconceived judgments based on the I.Q. stigma.

Lack of a Nongraded Model

It is important that teachers, administrators and parents have an opportunity to visit those schools which admit acceptance of the nongraded philosophy. Obviously, this provides the opportunity to see the concept in action, to judge advantages and disadvantages of certain components, to glimpse the future effectiveness of a comprehensive program and to observe pitfalls of procedure and methodology to be avoided. Generally speaking, it proves extremely beneficial to all concerned if numerous observation visits are made to various schools prior to implementation of a nongraded program. These visits also serve to focus awareness on the state of education today and on the overwhelming need for change which is often ignored through the complacency which arises from educational incest and provincialism.

Homogeneous Grouping

Many school districts fail to adequately meet the challenge of achieving a truly nongraded school because they homogenize classes with the result that teachers fall easily back into the old routine of educating groups — in this case, perhaps, smaller groups. While this would be fine if each child in each group received instruction and guidance according to his individual needs, all too often what actually happens is that each group of children is viewed as a whole in which all the children contained therein are alike. This, of course, merely represents a smaller lock-step, graded structure and we are well aware that small-class size alone is not synonymous with the development of the fullest potential of each individual child. Once teachers are committed to the nongraded philosophy, it is no longer necessary to force heterogeneity. This does not mean a return to homogeneous grouping, but it does allow greater flexibility to administrators and teaching staff in making up classes, particularly in the attempt to group according to interests.

Another objection to homogeneous grouping which effects nongraded education is cited by Dr. William P. McLaughlin in his assessment of nongraded schools:

> "When homogeneous grouping has been employed by any other name, even nongrading, it has failed to produce significant differences in the achievement or adjustment of boys and girls... We know from the amount of research available that homogeneous grouping is a very brittle proposition that does little or nothing to reduce individual differences and improve student performance."[3]

It is obvious from the foregoing that homogeneous grouping should not be the primary grouping procedure in a nongraded program.

Use of Academic Achievement Scores

Although each of the foregoing items might receive different weight, each is important in its own right, for the inclusion of a single one might constitute a severe drawback to an effective nongraded program.

The academic achievement score has a very limited place in the nongraded educational program. Schools that group students according to these scores are not practicing nongraded techniques. In the nongraded school, the only effective use of the academic achievement score involves its use as an evaluating instrument to determine the progress made by students in the entire school between the end of the traditional program and the implementation of the nongraded program, followed by periodic tests to record continuing progress. Ideally, the author would do away with even this aspect of the use of academic achievement scores but, unfortunately, until educators and parents arrive at the realization that grades and scores, per se, have no place in a truly humanistic program, the schools must continue to administer them to satisfy traditionally oriented persons with regard to the effectiveness of the nongraded program.

---

[3] William P. McLaughlin, *The Nongraded School – A Critical Assessment,* The University of the State of New York, The State Education Department, 1967, p. 39.

Identifying Levels by Grade

The mistake of using a system of level sequence identified by grade levels is often encountered. This technique enables teachers, in fact encourages them, to fall back into old habits of identifying levels by grades. We must studiously ostracize any system which leans toward the lock-step, grade-oriented program. A completely nongraded school with grade levels is as ineffective as it is semantically impossible, and can do nothing less than destroy the entire program.

Imperfect Classroom Organization

The nongraded school with its emphasis on individuality must, of necessity, concern itself with the physiological development of its students as well as their mental development, since one does affect the other. The concept of 50 uncomfortable seats in a drab room fronted by a gregarious teacher seated behind a foreboding desk in front of a blackboard backdrop must be banished. Classrooms and their contents must be rearranged so that they may easily accommodate flexibility in the curriculum and individualization of instruction, along with comfort and security for students and teachers individually, with students and teachers grouped in a team teaching approach, so as to assure the maximum in physical accommodation. The underlying idea was expressed succinctly in a particular classroom in one of the nongraded schools visited in which no teacher's desk or chair was visible. When the author inquired about this absence, the teacher responded: "Every student's chair is a teacher's chair."

Time-Honored Method of Instructing

The time-honored method of instructing innocent youth through the medium of lecturing over and over again to specified groups of children all studying, or rather listening to the same subject for the same amount of time, must be completely eradicated if the nongraded structure is to survive. This type of teaching is taboo but, because of ingrained discipline, the easiest to regress to. It is infamous that even today, most of our colleges and universities stoically adhere to this type of instruction which makes students into passive sounding boards, accepting what is fed into their ears, writing notes of meaningless jargon which they then memorize by rote to pass a course about which they often have little fundamental understanding.

Teacher Misunderstanding

It is of the utmost importance to the success of the program that teachers who are to implement a nongraded program be properly oriented as to the meaning of the nongraded concept and supplied with extensive background information about the nongraded philosophy, techniques and methods prior to undertaking the detailed planning and organization procedures. There should be a continuing series of frequent meetings between staff members to arouse their awareness of the need for use of the nongraded philosophy. This is especially true of experienced teachers who are completely indoctrinated to a pattern of traditional teaching methods, which makes it difficult to re-educate them to the concept of becoming sensitized to the individual needs of each child as opposed to the needs of a group of children. Concerted and intensive efforts on the part of administrators and fellow faculty members to guide, inform and share experiences with regard to living with the nongraded concept should not be overlooked or carelessly planned. The success of the entire staff of teachers in implementing the nongraded concept is, after all, dependent on each individual teacher working with her associates toward common goals. If this preliminary phase is well planned and implemented, the end result will be an eagerness on the part of teachers to initiate a nongraded program, and this is the only circumstance under which any school district should attempt to make the transition.

Unrealistic Testing Procedures

It is of vital importance, when testing or examining children in the traditional nongraded environment, that no time limitation be imposed on the students. No student should have to bear the burden of completing a test within a given period of time. Here, too, the individuality of each human being must be taken into account with the consideration of the fact that even as each will progress individually, each will also complete examinations in varying periods of time. Tests should also be presented so as to allow for individuality of response, for just as some individuals are capable of supplying short, comprehensive responses, others find it necessary to expound on several aspects before arriving at what is, after all, a correct conclusion.

Partial Nongraded Practices

An added drawback to effective implementation of the true nongraded plan is the tendency on the part of some schools to maintain what they refer to as "The Joplin Plan" of grouping children so as to utilize nongraded practices only in certain of the more difficult subject areas such as, for example, reading and mathematics. Certainly, if the nongraded concept proves effective with more difficult subject matter, its effectiveness in facile subject matter is preordained and, in the interests of providing the best education possible, an educator should be constrained by conscience to expand the nongrading to cover the entire curriculum.

Specified Number of Textbooks

One of the great culprits undermining the effectiveness of a nongraded plan, however, is the use of bi-basal or tri-basal textbooks by school administrators and educators. The continued adherence to a specified number of "basic" textbooks may stem from the reluctance of textbook manufacturers to relinquish the economic advantages of providing large numbers of self-same texts for millions of children. The iconoclastic nongraded school must be adamant in its refusal to accept large numbers of stereotyped texts which engird teachers rigidly and fail to play the important role that flexible texts are destined for in the purist approach to the nongraded concept. How can one even consider using identical textbooks for individualized instruction of pupils whose approaches to a subject differ, whose retention in varied areas differ, and whose interest levels run the gamut from intense to indifferent? Individualized texts must be used concomitantly with individualized instruction. The prohibitive expense to a school district might well be ameliorated by utilizing paperback texts to successfully achieve the necessary variety in approach, presentation and direction to more stylized learning. However, with regard to texts, extreme caution is urged in view of the publicized results of a recent National Education Association survey of teachers and administrators which established that some 65 percent of the subjects reflected a conviction that the textbook is the basic classroom tool. The flexibility which must be maintained in the curriculum of the nongraded school cancels any significance which the textbook might have had in centuries past as the basic educational tool.

Lack of Organized Nongraded Materials

One of the major problems in the effective implementation of the nongraded concept stems from the lack of organized materials to meet the needs of each identifiable level in every subject area. Allowance must be made for these materials concurrently with development of curriculum and the individual study units, if the nongraded program is to be successful.

Standardized Plan Book and Lesson Plans

Gone are the weekly or monthly lesson plans arranged by teachers in advance of meeting the students in their classes. Gone are the stereotyped lectures and lesson plans used over and over from one year of teaching to the next. What could be more sensible than for a teacher to interview and test her individual students to determine their levels of achievement, ability and interest before preparing a lesson plan which will be relevant? Within the nongraded context, day-to-day pre-plans, based on yesterday's class meeting, or yesterday's evaluation of individual progress signifies a timely and effective educational process.

Unfortunately, the author has observed that certain of the nongraded schools visited used a type of plan book devised for the entire class. Obviously, if we are thinking in terms of individuals — individualized instruction and individualized progress — there should be a plan book for each individual child. It has been broached that this would not be feasible. However, if we attack the problem in terms of revising the curriculum, and preparing individual study units, it would be both possible and feasible to include a curriculum plan guide for each youngster.

Lack of Pupil Profile Cards

Pupil Profile Cards should be designed and implemented by the elementary school teams as an added aid to effective organization. These cards permit efficiency by secretaries involved in the necessary process of compiling rosters of teams in each building, and provide key information to facilitate racial balance, sexual balance, and avoidance of concentrating what appear to be learning disabilities or emotional weaknesses in confined, segregated tracks. This completely eliminates homogenization and prevents an over-abundance of a specific type of problem within one class, while providing realistic measures to ensure heterogeneity in classrooms.

Audio-Visual Room

Many traditional school districts have set aside a small room in which audio-visual equipment is kept. Storing audio-visual equipment in a neglected "out of the way" room "down the hall" does nothing but provide a location for equipment to accumulate dust. This is not meant to imply that there should not be a place set aside especially for audio-visual equipment. To the contrary, there should be such a place, easily accessible, and located in the hub of school activities. The ideal way of doing this is to make provision for a resource center in which this equipment can be located for use by teachers and students. Teachers may be involved in service and maintenance of equipment, examination of materials, and review of student work. Students may be trained in the use of such equipment, its maintenance, and its comparative value in terms of the technological society in which they exist.

Lack of Pupil Orientation

Sensitive and efficient orientation of students constitutes one of the most vital elements in the nongraded program. Faculty conferences should be scheduled as part of careful administrative planning to explore areas and extent of information to be purveyed which will lead to appropriate teacher-pupil explanatory discussions. Uniformity in use of terms through the school district should be one essential, and another area of concentration should involve making certain that all concepts are couched in terms that will be readily understood by the students, without misinterpretation. Content should include ideas of individual challenge and independence which will inspire motivation. Each student should be made to realize that most of his successful achievement is the product of his own efforts and that he may forge as far ahead as he wishes to, regardless of his classmates' progress. In like manner, emphasis should be placed on the fact that completion of all the steps may take place within a period ranging from two to four years depending on the ability and effort of the individual student. It is important, too, to assure students that each one will have complete freedom to progress at his individual rate of speed in successfully completing each learning skill step, and that there will be no pressures either to speed up or slow down in order to match the efforts of some other student. The concept that the "failures" of traditional education are well-nigh non-existent in this program is obviously deserving of elaboration.

Lack of Parent and Community Orientation

It is essential that information and orientation be provided to parents so that they too may have full comprehension of the philosophy with which the public school is attempting to improve the education offered their children.

Several avenues of communication should be utilized to disseminate information to parents. Release to news media should be made with reference to approval by the Board of Education of the contemplated program. This should be immediately followed by a brief, formal letter from the chief school administrator referring to the forthcoming introduction of the program on a particular date. Subsequently, it is particularly effective if a spring meeting can be scheduled for parental attendance prior to initiation of the nongraded program. If it is impossible to do this, parent conferences should be scheduled as early as possible in the school year, and should occur periodically at frequent intervals during alternate daytime and evening hours to permit the most comprehensive parent coverage.

The preliminary conference should be attended by the principal and primary teachers for the purpose of making a well-informed and knowledgeable presentation of the philosophy and operational procedures involved in the program. Detailed emphasis should be placed on important aspects of the program, such as pupil progression, classroom grouping, team teaching, evaluation methods and reporting procedures. Attendance at this conference is also indicated for the chief school administrator in order that he may elaborate on district policy in conjunction with any questions which may arise. The program for the conference should make provision for ample time allotments for parental comments and a question and answer session. The success of the program may be greatly impaired without parental cooperation, so it is extremely important that parents are made to feel that their comments are welcomed and valued.

Subsequent parental meetings should be scheduled for discussion of the program's progress, appropriate means of evaluation, and any future plans. At these conferences it would be wise to include some film presentations, presentations by experts in the educational field, circulation of sample report forms and skill check lists, together with charts indicating individual group patterns of students as well as the academic progress of each student.

The importance of an effective public relations program between the school and the community must not be underestimated. However, publicity can be either an advantage or a disadvantage to the program and, therefore, all news releases, brochures or newsletters should be carefully planned, prepared and edited prior to dissemination. Efforts should also be made to involve local ministers and the administrators of local nursery schools by inviting them to attend any informative sessions or meetings that are being held. The school must, in effect, reach out into the community to place the objectives of the program in front of the eyes of the public so that all may achieve an easy and informed familiarity with it.

This familiarity will do more than anything else to ameliorate the ingrained habit of thinking and talking in terms of traditional grades.

Standardized Report Card

Within the nongraded system, the standardized report card with gradations of "excellent," "good," "fair," "poor," or varied alphabetical symbols, has no place as a determinant of the performance of any particular student. Unfortunately, this relic from the traditional age which is used by many school districts — among them, many supposedly nongraded schools — can have serious consequences. We know that what is "fair" for Mary may represent a concentrated effort at mastery which may, for Mary, be translated as a high level of achievement; while what is "excellent" for Jane may constitute only a mediocre performance well below what it might be possible for her to achieve, were the curriculum less restrictive and better tailored to her interests and abilities. Should Mary then be encouraged to emulate Jane? Should Jane then have a feeling of self-satisfaction in a job done well enough? Or is each not bound to be misled and confused as to her own true worth and esteem? We must discard permanently a theory that permits comparison of one child with another when each child, as an individual, should be compared only with himself, and led to compete only with himself.

Unfortunately, some nongraded schools still follow the practice of issuing to parents a standard card form to report the progress of offspring, while at the same time utilizing other admirable facets of the nongraded concept. Although it is true that progress must and should be recorded, analyzed and reviewed, the nongraded concept has no place for the old punishing stigma of failing individual students who are proceeding at their own rate. If we are truly converted to the theory of each child competing with himself, then the most satisfactory method of reporting progress would be within the sanctity of the dual conference; i.e., one conference with the child, the parent and the teacher participating. Complete reports should be kept of these conferences. A form of graph which will convey information as to the child's level of performance in various skills, the profoundness of his performance, and the amount of effort he is exerting, should be explored in detail at these meetings and should be retained in the child's permanent record for comparative analytic purposes at subsequent times.

Imperfect Organization

The successful structure of a nongraded program is dependent upon having, as a foundation, an organizational pattern which has been carefully planned by and is attentively administered by an administrative and professional staff. This applies to teacher organization as well as student organization. Nongraded teachers must participate in organization through the media of regular meetings for the purpose of constantly reviewing their ideas, plans and methods.

These meetings constitute a focal point which provides for growth and enhancement in the operation of the nongraded program by the team. A useful element in this connection is the appointment of a thoroughly knowledgeable member of the staff as a team leader who can serve as a resource person to aid, advise and guide the group in solution of particular problems. Students, too, must be organized to some extent. It is important to bear in mind the fact that, depending on age and maturation, it usually takes students approximately three to six weeks to become oriented to the procedures involved in the new nongraded program. This factor alone can be instrumental in determining the success or failure of the program.

Needless to say, there is also a distinct need for methods which provide flexible organization for teaching in the schools and which are an improvement over the traditional school schedule. Although we will not elaborate here on what is a very comprehensive plan, the concept of Modular Scheduling, which entails the division of the instructional day into "modules" of time which vary in length according to the particular needs of differentiated facets of the nongraded program, would seem to present a modern solution to organizational problems. In effect, Modular Scheduling tailors the organization of the school to the needs of the students, teachers, and instructional program. With the use of Modular Scheduling, time may be allocated with primary consideration given to inequality of necessary time for mastery of particular subjects and alterations in class size pertinent to needs of students and teachers. The Modular Scheduling concept was developed by Dr. K. Lloyd Trump.

Unrealistic Teaching Schedule

Teachers in a nongraded classroom are only human beings with certain limitations. Because they are human beings with individual differences, interests, and proficiencies, it is arbitrarily perverse to confine a teacher in the same classroom, teaching all subjects as though she were equally proficient in all of them. For example, it is elemental that a teacher who may be highly competent in the language arts may be weak in arithmetic, and this principle may be expanded to all other areas of subject matter in this age of specialization.

If we are here extolling the virtue of a program geared to the ability and interest level of each child, then we must also seek a realistic teaching schedule geared to the interests and proficiency of the teacher. If this is not taken into account, we run the risk of prematurely burning out the nongraded teacher with 25 to 30 individual groups on a modular schedule which makes for a total of approximately 150 groups per day. Team teaching provides the obvious solution to these problems, while expanding the teacher horizon to include all pupils and all classrooms to some extent so that perspectives may be broadened from the possessive "my class" and "my desk," to include "my school" and "my students."

No Panacea

While there is really no panacea which will effectively nongrade all schools, it is possible to avoid the most obvious of the above pitfalls which can signal disaster for the program. Administrators and teachers would do well to keep a weather eye on the classroom atmosphere and the students themselves as part of the evaluation of the success of any nongraded program. For example, in the nongraded classes there should be an impression of ample space, a bustle of activity, and a warm, intimate atmosphere in which students are pursuing their activities with a minimum of regimentation and strict supervision. Students should give the appearance of being intensely interested in the activity of the moment with self-confidence in what they are doing, why they are doing it, and the results they expect to achieve. Quite often, in the successful nongraded classroom, a classroom visitor is accorded only a cursory glance by students in groups, alone, at tables, or in study carrels, all of whom are under the mesmeric influence of learning according to their capabilities and interests.

A Parallel Example

Education, if it is going to be truly effective, must be presented in a humane manner. The pitfalls cited above are enumerated to avert the depersonalizing which results in alienation and frustration in the educational process. It seems appropriate at this terminal point of the chapter to list a number of items which were cited by a committee responsible for the composition of the 1962 Yearbook of the Association for Supervision and Curriculum Development as being practices which contributed to alienation and depersonalization.

. . . The emphasis on fact instead of feelings

. . . The belief that intelligence is fixed and immutable

. . . The continual emphasis upon grades, artificial reasons instead of real ones for learning

. . . Conformity and preoccupation with order and neatness

. . . Authority, support and evidence

. . . Solitary learning

. . . Cookbook approaches

. . . Adult concepts as the only ones of value

. . . Emphasis on competition

. . . Lockstep progression

. . . Force, threat and coercion

. . . Wooden rules and regulations

. . . The age-old idea that if it's hard, it's good for them

A close observation of the above items will reveal a true parallel between the pitfalls cited on the foregoing pages and those items cited by the ASCD.

As a rule, any procedure, any technique, any plan, or any program which tends to depersonalize the instructional program is a pitfall and must be avoided when implementing not only the nongraded program, but any educational program which is meant to be effective. The goal of contemporary education, nongraded education, must be viewed much as a process of resurrection, of breathing new life and warmth into the deathlike coldness of education.

SUMMARY

The primary reason for the fact that so many school districts fail to implement a successful nongraded program lies in the virtual non-existence of specific guidelines for nongrading. There is simply no strict rule of thumb to follow in making a successful transition from traditional education to nongraded education. However, while there are no specified "do's," there are some very definite "dont's," as indicated in this chapter, which should be avoided at all costs. If the elements of humanism and individualism are going to be made an integral part of the public school system, a well-defined avoidance technique with respect to the pitfalls listed herein can add immeasurably to the success of the nongraded program which is otherwise adequately structured.

3. IMPLICATIONS OF THE NONGRADED CONCEPT FOR THE CULTURALLY DIFFERENT CHILD

Slum environment handicaps a child educationally almost from birth. The growing child in this environment does not receive the necessary prerequisites to formal schooling, intellectual and sensory stimulation.

Arthur B. Shostak

The graded school was established in the nineteenth century when very little was known about individual differences in youngsters, with the exception of those views promulgated by far-thinking men such as John Dewey and a few others. The educational philosophy at that time dictated that the instructional program be divided into equal segments to be mastered by children of the same age. Added impetus to this view was given by publication firms who catered to the graded system of classes by publishing graded textbooks and materials. Before long, everything related to school had to be "graded." As a consequence, we ended up with "graded children," "grade teachers," "graded tests" and "graded report cards." Within a relatively short time, the graded philosophy was well entrenched in the very fibers of our public and private school systems. At that time, it may be that the graded system was efficient in instilling an adequate education in the minds of those children who entered the portals of the public school system from a much less complex society than we have today. Then, perhaps, the quality of the education offered was appropriate to captivate the public school student and keep him in school for the required years. However, the twentieth century public school system, which has fostered a high rate of attrition in schools where "graded" education is the norm, points to the need for investigation and analysis of individual youngsters in order to provide educational programs which can improve academic achievement in school. This looms particularly true in the case of the culturally different children who may come to public school from the poverty stricken Appalachian area; who may be a member of an ethnic minority sub-culture such as the Puerto Rican, Mexican or black child; or who may be a member of a vanishing culture such as the American Indian. For these children, particularly, the far-reaching effects of an unsuccessful preparatory education are obvious when consideration is taken of the fact that they comprise a total of more than ten million young Americans. The graded system of education has been and must, of necessity, continue to be ineffective for these youngsters because it thrives on certain basic ingredients which serve only to thwart their aspirations, i.e.:

1. It assumes that all children of the same age are alike and, consequently, should be able to master a certain amount of material within a certain specified time.

2. It assumes that each child who enters the public schools has been socialized in the white, middle class tradition.

3. It assumes that children who do not achieve within its rigidly prescribed limitations are incapable of achieving.

4. It assumes that children who demonstrate an ability to successfully cope with its limitations, and seek to acquire more knowledge than the grade prescribes, are over-achievers and must be stifled.

5. It assumes that all children will benefit from a system of "rewards and punishment" evidenced by an abstract "grade" of "A" for implied perfection which, of course, is never present in any student who is in the process of learning; or the equally abstract "F" grade which implies that a student is a total failure and must repeat everything in the course.

6. It assumes that in the learning process repetition is as important as arousal of interest and curiosity.

7. It assumes that although it is obviously not effectively educating a portion of its students, the failure is to be attributed to some innate flaw in the students and no radical change need be made in its processes.

One of the subcultural elements which tend to handicap culturally different children in their ability to achieve under programs of traditional education is pointed up by Arthur B. Shostak:

> For example, the deprived child frequently has an under-developed ability to distinguish subtle differences and nuances in sound. This auditory handicap is a regular cost of crowded living conditions, city noises, regional dialects, and restricted vocabularies. The handicap makes learning to read much more difficult, as does also the youngster's poor attention span, his difficulty in following directions, his untrained memory, limited perception, poor motivation, and physical restlessness.[1]

Not only is the culturally different child handicapped by this myriad of deterrents to learning, but all too often he may be assigned to a teacher who is insensitive to his problems, and who may herself be a victim of cultural shock upon being exposed to the differences in children who do not have a solid middle class background akin to her own. Mr. Shostak's remarks have been substantiated by Charles E. Silberman's statement that:

> Mental alertness and, in particular, the ability to handle abstractions depends physiologically on a broad diversity of experience in the environment of early childhood.[2]

This "broad diversity of experience" in the early childhood environment is conspicuously absent in the lives of culturally different children. For children who come from ghetto neighborhoods, a large amount of the early training, experiences and

---

[1] Arthur B. Shostak and William Gomberg, "Educational Reforms and Poverty," *New Perspectives on Poverty* (Englewood Cliffs: Prentice-Hall, Inc., 1965), p. 63.

[2] Charles E. Silberman, *Crisis in Black and White* (New York: Random House, Inc., 1964), p. 273.

observations with which a middle or upper class child usually comes to school is lacking. The culturally different child is rudely thrust into an alien world where authority figures speak, look and act differently than those to which he is accustomed; where the activities he is introduced to are unlike any of those he has been exposed to in his home; and where he is expected to absorb the same amount of material that all of his classmates do, or risk the ignominy of failure coupled with the boredom of repeating unintelligible material. These children, more than any others, need the benefits of an educational program which is intensive and extensive, striving toward excellence rather than mediocrity, if they are to realize the upward social mobility that our system of public education is meant to nurture.

The homes of such children are filled with poverty whose tentacles encircle everything within reach. Walls are usually bare of the paintings which inspire the "why" questions and round out visual experiences. Books and toys meant especially for a small child to begin his learning are considered "unnecessary luxuries." Parents and other authority figures exhibit hopeless attitudes of resignation which the child, in his early imitative years, begins to copy. For the child whose curiosity is overwhelming, frequent questioning turns up only a monosyllabic answer from a tired parent intent on the struggle for survival, or a physical blow coupled with an admonishment. This child soon learns to stop asking questions and to bury his questing spirit. Auditory perceptions and discrimination dulled by ghetto noises and monosyllabic conversations are further burdens which the culturally different child brings to school. In many of these homes, there is not even a mirror so that the child may see an image of his physical self, and these children do not usually identify with the "outsiders" they see on the world of the television screen.

These culturally different students can be taught, however, if the educators can combine sensitivity, skill, imagination, patience, respect and love, all of which are basic ingredients of a humanistic approach to educating all children. Unfortunately, most of these ingredients are generally absent in traditional educational programs. Actually, the design of traditional education works to levy an additional hardship on all culturally different children. The cultural deprivation existing in the homes of these children is a great handicap, and they are subjected to yet another handicap inherent in the organizational pattern of the public school system where one teacher, usually middle class oriented, is responsible for teaching some 30 of these culturally different children as though all were alike, mentally, physically, emotionally, academically, and in terms of interest levels. Attempts have been made to compensate for the restrictive uniformity of the graded system through mediums such as remedial classes, continuous promotion, field visits, tutoring programs, elimination of de facto segregation, and compensatory education. However, these attempts only serve to emphasize the fact that something is wrong with the present graded system, without really correcting the inherent problems. The potential harm in traditional education is partially evidenced by the high dropout rate which is calculated at more than 50 percent; by the poor self-image fostered in the culturally different child because of the failure he receives and consequent retention; and by the eruption of an entirely new vocabulary to label him as " a non-achiever," "disruptive," "a slow learner" and "pseudo mentally retarded," all of which terms tend to further stigmatize the culturally different child and reinforce his feelings of inadequacy. Therefore, the culturally different child has several strikes against him when he reaches the required age for entrance to public school and, upon entering the portals of the public school, receives additional bludgeoning.

Nongradedness in Early Childhood Education

Some reflection is indicated in terms of general, realistic and practical solutions to the inadequacies of the education received by a culturally different child today. The report of the President's National Advisory Commission on Civil Disorders vividly states some of the guidelines which might be followed in initiating an assault on some of the inadequacies:

> Early Childhood Education programs should provide comprehensive educational support tailored to the needs of the child, and should not be simply custodial care. Both day care and Head Start components are part of comprehensive early childhood education; each should be designed to overcome the debilitating effect on learning ability of a disadvantaged environment.

> Parents and the home environment have a critical impact on a child's early development. Early childhood programs should involve parents and the home, as well as the child. This can be accomplished through community education classes, and use

of community aides and mother's assistants. To reduce the incidence of congenital abnormalities, these community-based programs should be tied in with prenatal training.

Since adequate facilities are scarce in many disadvantaged communities, where schools are overcrowded, and buildings deteriorated, the program should provide funds for special early childhood education facilities.

There is a need for maximum experimentation and variety. Funding should continue to support early childhood programs operated by community groups and organizations, as well as by the school system.

Early childhood education programs should include provisions for medical care and food, so that the educational experience can have its intended impact.[3]

Many states in the nation have initiated programs for early childhood education beginning with children as young as three years. However, education cannot come too early and it might well be advocated that some elements of early childhood education begin as soon as the child reaches one year of age. This attitude is supported by the Infant Education Program proposed by the Public Schools of the District of Columbia. The program was based on generalizations supported by research on intellectual development during the pre-school years which suggested that:

> ... we should move toward the development of infant education programs to supplement the efforts of parents who do not have the skills or resources to provide the positive relationships, varied experiences, and verbal stimulation that is necessary for rapid intellectual development during this critical period of early verbal development.

The program was a design for an infant education project that would utilize parents, high school students, and a central educational staff to foster the intellectual development of approximately 280 infants. The central staff would be responsible for training the parents and students as infant educators, thereby raising the level of intellectual functioning of the infants while, at the same time, increasing the level of involvement and effectiveness in infant

---

[3] *The Report of the President's National Advisory Commission on Civil Disorders,* New York Times Co., 1968, p. 446-447.

education of the participating parents and high school students. Unfortunately, the project never evolved past the planning stage.

The most appropriate educational design for an effective early childhood program exists in the nongraded environment, primarily because its individualized methods make ample allowance for the differences in children. These differences are readily discernible, especially at this early age where a comparison of age-mates will show that some are able to read short sentences and others cannot; that one speaks in complete sentences while the other does not; and where some work very well in the semi-structured atmosphere while others must have more time in which to adjust. Obviously, the only commonsense program must be one that is highly individualized.

The play-academic program for culturally different youngsters should be individualized. These youngsters should be placed on a level, designated by letters of the alphabet, to indicate their physical, mental and social maturation and readiness to enter the basic educational program. In the preliminary stages of formal education, kindergarten is omitted, because the author believes that kindergarten rightfully should be included in the early childhood program of education. When a child completes all necessary levels in the early childhood program, he should be permitted to proceed immediately to an academically oriented program, regardless of his age, as some are ready to start at four years and some only reach readiness at five, six or seven years of age.

Nongraded Education in the Elementary and Secondary Schools

A number of schools have implemented the nongraded concept on the primary level and we applaud this because, in essence, the primary grades should lay the foundation for a successful educational career. Obviously, if a child has unsuccessful experiences at the primary level, the negative stimuli received during this critical period will influence his performance and behavior in the intermediate school, and by the time he reaches the high school level his problems will have been compounded. If we are to agree on the necessity for establishing the nongraded concept of education with individualized instruction in the primary grades, then we must also concur on its necessity at all succeeding grade levels, even through the college level.

The major mechanical and technical steps which should be undertaken to supplement the educator's humanistic approach to education are clearly delineated in the Report of the President's National Advisory Commission on Civil Disorders:

> Without major changes in educational practices, greater expenditures on existing elementary schools serving disadvantaged neighborhoods will not significantly improve the quality of education. Moreover, current assessments of pre-school programs indicate that their gains are lost in the elementary grades, unless the schools themselves are improved.[4]

The most practical, realistic and human way to effect the major changes referred to is implementation of the nongraded philosophy in the basic educational program.

The nongraded school heralds a significant benefit to the culturally different child whose history can be traced through a series of failures in lower grades, followed by disinterest in achievement and a high rate of eventual dropping out.

Concerned educators have long realized the existence of, but have only recently begun to adopt measures to correct and compensate for, the basic deficiencies with which the culturally different child arrives at school. Originally, the nongraded system has been made available in large measure to children attending private schools. Obviously, the need for this specialized method is far greater in the public schools whose entrants have not had and, indeed, may never have individualized instruction applied to their special needs. Individualized instruction under the nongraded system will quickly assess each child's maximum and minimum disadvantage so that weak areas may receive full concentration very early in the school career. The child who sometimes represents just another burden to the ghetto family, is transformed into someone special by the teacher who works with him on his individual problems, permitting him to proceed at his own level of achievement without humiliating comparisons to a classmate who is further advanced, and without the failing marks on the end term report which signify another term of doing the same work over again which, by now, has a distinctly onerous quality.

---

[4] The Report of the President's National Advisory Commission on Civil Rights Disorders, N. Y. Times Co., 1968, p. 447.

The individualized attention given to each child will serve to raise the child's concept of self as he more often experiences success in his efforts rather than failure. Team teaching methods will allow the in-depth instruction some pupils benefit from without placing a burden of "keeping up" on all pupils. The experience with success in the nongraded system of individual progress often provides the impetus for competitive attempts at higher achievement. Flexible scheduling, high interest, multi-level instructional materials, and opportunities for independent study can lengthen the short attention span of most of these children, equipping them with a sincere interest in learning and giving birth to new feelings of self-confidence and self-determination.

A Private Nongraded School
for the Culturally Different Child

One of the most successful examples of humanism at work in a nongraded school may be observed by visiting the Harlem Prep School on Eighth Avenue in New York City. The success of the Harlem Prep School with its student population of dropouts ranging in age from 16 to 49 is incontrovertible proof of the failure of traditional education.

The academic program at Harlem Prep encompasses the four subject areas of social studies, African culture, mathematics, and English. Classes are conducted in an informal manner, utilizing small and medium group instruction where students are grouped around a table, or aligned in movable chairs encircling the instructor, with a portable blackboard standing nearby ready to be rolled into use. Students are constantly afforded opportunities to participate in their own learning and the learning of other students. For instance, in English classes, students write essays which are then read before the class so that all class members may participate in correcting, modifying, and evaluating the papers. A great deal of relevance is incorporated into the curriculum through the use of contemporary, paperback texts which bear relevance to the students' life-realities, such as *An Autobiography of Malcolm X, The Confessions of Nat Turner* and *W.A.S.P.S.* etc. These texts serve to encourage the growth of reading habits, and all preliminary texts are black-oriented to arouse interest and increase motivation among students to read regularly. Most classes are composed of no more than 10 to 15 students. The class in African culture is conducted by an African and, since all students participate in this course, medium group instruction is usually relied upon.

Among most students and instructors, adherence to the new "black image" is readily apparent in the pride with which au naturelle hair styles, jewelry, and clothing which reflect the influence of Africa are worn. Each instructor discusses and presents his materials with a distinctive air of intimacy and informality. Those students needing further clarification of a point casually direct their comments to instructors, and instructors reply in the tones of a one-to-one relationship, in which other students voluntarily become involved.

This school is housed in what was formerly a large supermarket, and which is being converted to accommodate an increased enrollment. At Harlem Prep all students are allowed to progress at their own pace, and the emphasis placed on the dignity and human worth of each individual has contributed immensely to the high motivation which is evident among its students. All identification with traditional forms of public education has been cast out in this unique school where hungry students are allowed to eat in class; sleepy students are not embarrassed or penalized for dozing in class; and students need not ask permission to retire to a rest room to attend to personal needs. The students' response to being treated as human beings is to react as human beings and, as a result, they do not abuse the humane conditions under which they are permitted to learn. Harlem Prep exists in the middle of a large urban ghetto and most of its students are Afro-Americans who come from socially, economically, or psychologically disadvantaged backgrounds. Many of these students have been "forced out" of the public school system, but all are still trying to acquire the education necessary for coping with the society in which they live. So, they come to Harlem Prep where classes are small and imbued with relevance to the life-realities of these students. At Harlem Prep, they find sensitive and well-trained instructors who are extremely flexible and create many-faceted approaches to arouse and maintain student interest. There is a free flow of communication between teachers in different subject areas so that students are presented with an inter-disciplinary approach to learning. In addition, each teacher is expected to and does serve not only as instructor, but also as friend, guidance counselor and advisor.

A private school, made possible by grants from the Carnegie Corporation and other foundations and business corporations, Harlem Prep is staffed by a cadre of Marymount Sisters and professionals with degrees ranging from the Masters to the Doctorate. Moreover, the school maintains a long waiting list of outstanding instructors who would like to have the opportunity of participating in the learning process at this unique school. If college entrance is to be considered as the determinant of success of a school like Harlem Prep, then Harlem Prep ranks among the top. In 1967-68, all of its 36 graduating students were accepted into some of the best institutions for higher learning in the United States, including Berkeley College, Buffalo University, Fordham University, Vassar College, Wesleyan University, Long Island University, SUNY Stony Brook and Harvard University. In addition, 20 of these students were surveyed after the first semester of studies and the majority were found to have maintained grade averages of A to B, with the lowest mark received being a C+. What makes Harlem Prep work? Perhaps the best reason can be found in the words of the school's director, Mr. Carpenter: "Every kid in this school gets warmth, affection and love – and they give it, too."

Sensitizing Teachers

Keeping in mind the humanistic approach to education for the culturally different child, a major step must be taken before and during the implementation of the nongraded program. This step involves what is known as sensitivity training for all teachers of culturally different children. John H. Fischer in his essay entitled *School Programs*, stated the need quite succinctly:

> In dealing with a population which is racially and culturally integrated, the school must begin by encouraging teachers to understand the special factors in the backgrounds of all their children, to take these differences imaginatively into account, and to build curricula and teaching techniques that reflect not only idealism but realism as well.[5]

However, in order to do this effectively, primary steps must be taken by a teacher to understand himself, that is, to know himself,

---

[5] A. Harry Passow, *Education in Depressed Areas*, Teachers College, Columbia University Press, 1963, p. 293.

his possible prejudicial feelings, and other personality traits and attitudes which have a direct bearing upon his relationships with other human beings. Until and unless a teacher becomes highly sensitized to other human beings, any attempt to make humanism an essential ingredient in education is bound to fail. Sensitivity training, which is a form of experience-based learning, can be accomplished through well-planned sensitivity sessions. In this manner, it is possible for the teacher to increase his understanding of the many factors which influence his behavior which, in turn, influences the performances and reactions of other individuals. The sessions are best accomplished within the mechanical structure of a small, intimate group exploration guided by a sensitive psychoanalytically trained leader over an extended period of time. The acquisition of sensitivity is acquired by each participant through deep analysis of the individual's personal experiences which include emotions, perceptions, and behavioral reactions. The author attended a sensitivity marathon which lasted for 27 hours and his own personal reaction that it was one of the most rewarding experiences of his life may, perhaps, best be evidenced by the following excerpt from a letter he addressed to the psychoanalyst:

> I was deeply moved and, I believe, changed by the session. At the beginning of the meeting when surface conversations were going on and people were identifying themselves in various ways, I was extremely conscious of a void between each individual present, keeping them separate and apart, as creatures who presented an enigma to each other despite their common bond as members of the race of man ... When I left the meeting, I was imbued with a mental perceptivity which had some of the elements of tactile communication, if that is possible, and I felt that the most objectionable thing any of us who had been present might do would be to return to our private, outside worlds and deny the sensitivity exposed during the session. There are far too many humans in our society who are desensitized to desperate communications from other humans, so I felt it important that we, who had been exposed to the naked humanity of each individual present, retain and bring all of our feelings of sensitivity back into our immediate worlds ... I believe the entire session served to provide me with a sharper insight, which allows me to react somewhat differently to other humans.

The reader should be aware, however, that all sensitivity training sessions may or may not be as effective as others. A great deal of the success or failure of such sessions usually rests with the experience and qualifications of the persons in charge. The more experienced the "leader," the more effective his techniques will be for arousing the participants in the sensitivity training session. Among some of the more qualified sensitivity training persons are:

Dr. Leonard Schwartz, Director
Institute for Sensitivity Training
Brightwaters, New York
(Dr. Schwartz is also a clinical
professor at Adelphi University)

Dr. Charles Raebeck, Director
Teacher Education Program
Dowling College (Adelphi-Suffolk College)
Garden City, New York

Dr. Elizabeth Longhams, Professor
Education Department
Dowling College (Adelphi-Suffolk College)
Garden City, New York

Dr. Harold Greenwald, President
National Psychological Association
for Psychoanalysis

Dr. Joan Fagan, Director
Psychological Institute of Atlanta, Georgia
Atlanta, Georgia

Mrs. Roslyn Schwartz
Psychologist and Seniority Trainer
Brightwaters, New York

It must also be recognized that an administrator or faculty member who becomes sensitized will not necessarily change his views about people completely and/or immediately. Therefore, the extended sensitivity training institute outlined below, which was designed by the author in conjunction with staff members of the Institute for Sensitivity Training for a group of administrators proved to be most effective:

The function of an educational system as it pertains to the fulfillment of the individual, his society and the humanistic values held by both was discussed in broad as well as specific terms. The focus was on the individual – both pupil and teacher – and how to aid in the fullest development of each. The use of nongraded classes, children of various ages placed in each class, custom-designed curricula, the elimination of I.Q. reporting to teachers, de-emphasizing content teaching, and sensitivity training for teachers and administrators as well as parents and students were all considered as part of an over-all program to make Wyandanch a model educational system. Our sights were on the means by which we could help arouse and stimulate those personal resources that will enable teachers to develop within themselves and their pupils a positive self-image, and the freedom to launch those creative abilities that are presently bound up.

Sensitivity training was stressed as the most rapid means by which individuals can reach an immediate awareness of their inner states – physical, ideational, as well as emotional. Such training will enable the participants to become more familiar with that internal reality that seeks expression in the world around them. The encounter and confrontation techniques that are employed in this experience are designed to liberate and effectively direct the human potential within us all. Through a gradual increase in personal awareness, the participant learns to respect his feelings and thoughts and to design creative ways of expressing them effectively. Here the distinction between pupil and teacher is minimized as it becomes instantly clear that to become an effective teacher one must genuinely learn from the student. Specific sensitivity techniques are demonstrated and all participants are encouraged to innovate and design new avenues for the fullest expression of the human experience. In order to offer to the Wyandanch Public School System an organized program to achieve this end, the following types of Workshops were suggested to be used in combination for the fullest value to the educational program.

I. All Day Workshop

Designed for an intense and intimate involvement of 15 participants and two leaders in a comfortable setting away from the school. This initial experience focuses on individual sensitivity to internal reality, a respect for this self, and the beginnings of a sense of confidence that such experiences can be gratifying with positive results for all.

II. In-Service Training Course

This weekly four-hour meeting for four weeks emphasizes the internal uniqueness of each participant. This course is designed to provide an intense emotional setting in which participants will both experience and learn techniques and methods of bringing about instant encounter and confrontation. In an interactional group, members are asked to examine themselves – their own values, educational assumptions, and methods of working with children. They will be encouraged to expand their teaching horizons; to focus on the affective human, emotionally; to teach without using words; to function directionlessly; to get the pupil to lead in the search for a solution to a living problem; to respect the polar sizes of every situation; and to develop the courage and confidence to be flexible enough to experience the unknowns of life.

III. Intensive Departmental Encounter

This sensitivity experience is designed to aid the members of a working department to arrive at a greater affective and personally rewarding cooperative interchange in their daily work. Each member separately attends an intensive marathon group and is encouraged to feel the power of the use of his own individuality. Effectiveness, productivity, efficiency, and goal direction are pinned down as most attainable through a focus upon and the full utilization of one's personal resources. The typical problem of departmental structure versus individual expression disappears as the participant perceives the loss of the "they" – "I" dichotomy. He returns to his department confident that he is capable of "making it" through being himself regardless of departmental structure. After all members have individually attended a marathon group, a weekend workshop is designed for the entire departmental staff. Here, forthrightness, honesty and authenticity are shown to be the key routes towards harmonious and effective departmental achievement. Differences of opinion, competitiveness, jealousy, envy, and a host of other would-be negative reactions are opened up, explored, and utilized to arrive at a smoothly functioning team approach to problem solving. The respect for individual differences is honored at the outset and shown to be the basis for all human progress.

IV. Custom-Designed Workshop

A theme-centered workshop can be custom designed to fit any particular need of the school system as it arises.

As is obvious, the Institute was predicated on an attempt to sensitize administrators, supervisors, teachers, students and parents for the purpose of accomplishing, to one degree or another, the sensitization of an entire community of 11,000 people. Although this plan may have been in defiance of the objective realism which is a counterpart of so much of the current thinking about what may or may not be the best way to solve the ever-recurring problem of human differences which lead to dissension, it was felt that shooting for the moon and achieving something less would not be entirely amiss and would, to the contrary, serve a most useful purpose for those affected by the training. For, in the final analysis, the author would be gratified if only a few educators began to see themselves clearly for the first time and to reach the conclusion that if any child doesn't learn, it is rarely the fault of the child but, most often, the fault of the teacher or of the techniques used. An educator who finds it possible to think in these terms is well along the way toward exhibiting a truly humanistic approach to education.

A New Chance in School

In a nongraded environment, the culturally different child receives another chance in school. His life in school begins to be attuned to an educational climate which provides him with an equal opportunity to learn. His life, in this setting, will be constructively planned so that he will reap the benefits of a totally new world — the nongraded classroom. No longer will he fear being retained in the same grade because he could not comprehend the subject matter, or because the teacher failed to teach the subject matter in a manner suited to his needs. In this new world, an attempt is made to abolish failure as an educational concept. Instead, success is the area of concentration. This is accomplished by the implementation of a program which provides sufficient flexibility to meet the individual needs of each child. No longer will the culturally different child be labeled as "disruptive," "slow," or "unmanageable." In this new world, he will find an environment rich in a variety of educational tools. If one does not suit his taste, others can be employed so that his needs and interests can be met and fulfilled. He will cease being disruptive because he will begin to enjoy learning experiences in this new world. No longer will the culturally different student have to endure reprimands, punishment of weighty assignments, or even failure because of some acts of omission or commission. In this new world, he will not have the uncommitted time to become disruptive − he will be too busy enjoying learning to become disruptive and, consequently, to become a problem. No longer will the culturally different child be forced to sit in a class, tense, insecure and frustrated because of the rigidity of traditional education and the inhuman demands made on students in these classrooms. In this new world, the atmosphere is relaxed, yet busy and sometimes noisy with constructive noise heightened by gaiety over the successes found in learning. No longer will the culturally different child have to worry about keeping up with others in his class. In this new world he need only worry about keeping up with himself. No longer will the culturally different child fear teachers who are insensitive to his needs, interests, or abilities. In this new world, he has a humane, sensitive person to give him the care that he deserves and needs − he has a nongraded teacher. No longer will the culturally different child remain away from school for long periods of time or seek to escape to a more pleasant world of daydreams while he is physically in the classroom. In this new world, learning and success are synonymous and each day is a day to behold anew − a day to receive praise and a day to give praise - a day to learn and a day to teach - a day to care and a day to be cared for - a day to love and a day to be loved. This is that exciting new world of the nongraded classroom.

SUMMARY

The culturally different children with their special needs and, quite often, special talents to be developed, must have an educational program which approaches and encompasses the multifaceted areas of their interests, abilities and experiences. We now know that the solution does not lie in simply thrusting them into the middle class milieu and assuming they will absorb these educational offerings. We must provide them with the kind of education that recognizes their cultural differences while it capitalizes on their strengths and builds up their weaknesses.

4. INITIATING THE NONGRADED PROGRAM

If the development of an ungraded program is to be undertaken by a school or school district, it should be recognized that the success of the endeavor will be determined largely by the content and the quality of the preparatory activity.

Frank R. Dufay

The nongraded concept is difficult to implement, as well as difficult to maintain in practice. Part of these difficulties stem from the fact that, as yet, colleges and universities which train teachers have not begun to impart the skills necessary to organize a nongraded class. The available literature on the subject of nongradedness is also insufficient, and much of that which does exist is too inconsistent to enable a teacher fully to comprehend the most efficient ways and means of organizing her classroom for a program of individualized instruction. A further flaw lies in those educators credited with expertise who, in actuality, are giving only lip service to the nongraded concept. With all of these strikes operating against the teacher who seeks to implement the nongraded concept, it is no wonder that most teachers are confused as to the best direction to take in order to achieve success in meeting the individual needs of students. It is necessary for each teacher to begin building from the ground up in order to make sure she overlooks nothing in the process of implementing the nongraded program. The groundwork, which constitutes the foundation of a successful nongraded program, includes all the preparatory activities which are to be initiated in order to plan an effective educational program. Unless serious consideration is given to it prior to initiating what seems to be appropriate action, the items cited below can at once determine the success or failure of a nongraded program.

Collection of Nongraded Materials

In order to successfully initiate a nongraded program, it is incumbent upon the superintendent, the district principal, or the principal of the building in which the nongraded concept is going to be implemented, to become thoroughly familiar with all articles, books, magazines, and other printed materials on the subject of individualizing instruction.

School districts throughout the nation should be solicited for transmittal of all available materials which they have dealing with individualizing instruction. If this is successfully done, the chief administrator of the program may amass a vast library to serve as a tool which is readily available for reference. Needless to say, it is important that all of these materials be made available to all faculty members involved in the implementation and maintenance of the nongraded concept.

Visits to Nongraded Schools

Frequent and extensive visitations should be made, both locally and nationwide, to all schools purporting to be nongraded, for the purpose of observing and investigating these practices which would prove most effective in the school planning such transformation. Wherever and whenever possible, it is recommended that parents in the community be afforded an opportunity to visit these schools accompanied by teachers of the school districts. During these visits, teachers should make it a point to discuss with professional persons at the schools visited some of the problems encountered, their successful solution, and innovative activities undertaken. The visiting teachers should be extremely receptive to new things which are going on at these schools, taking along, if possible, cameras and recording instruments so they may share the information they have acquired with their fellow staff members. While at these schools, it would be wise, if the opportunity presents itself, for teachers to speak with students in the schools visited to ascertain their reactions to the nongraded program, their attitudes toward the school and toward their teachers since the inception of the nongraded program. At this point, the author is reminded of a reply received from a third grader in a school he visited to the question of how she felt about her multi-graded class. She stated: "I can always get one of the older children to help me."

Time should be reserved for a conference with the principal of the nongraded school to ascertain his philosophy, his procedures, his evaluation, his perspectives for the future, and a request should be made for any materials he might have available. It is important to remember that it is impossible to accumulate too much material.

The following is a partial list of recommended nongraded schools and schools initiating nongraded practices:

Elementary

1. Nova Elementary School
   Fort Lauderdale, Florida

2. Newton Public School System
   Newton, Massachusetts

3. Milton L. Olive Elementary School
   Wyandanch, New York

4. Hampton Nongraded Institute Laboratory School
   Hampton, Virginia

5. The University Elementary School of the
   University of California
   Los Angeles, California

6. Oakleaf Elementary School
   Pittsburgh, Pennsylvania

Secondary

1. Nova High School
   Fort Lauderdale, Florida

2. Melbourne High School
   Melbourne, Florida

3. Newton Public School System
   Newton, Massachusetts

4. Ridgewood High School
   Norridge, Illinois

5. Wheatland Chili Central School
   Scottsville, New York

6. Amherst High School
   Amherst, Massachusetts

7. Harlem Prep School
   New York City, New York

8. John Dewey High School
   Brooklyn, New York

9. Chester Park School
   Duluth Public Schools
   Duluth, Minnesota

Nongraded Workshops

Another useful preparatory tool with regard to implementation of a nongraded program is attendance at one or several nongraded workshops. Science Research Associates, Inc., frequently sponsors nongraded conferences and workshops throughout the United States, at which noted experts appear to give presentations which are followed by question and answer sessions. These workshops can be extremely beneficial to educators being introduced to the nongraded concept. In addition, a number of colleges and universities have sponsored nongraded conferences in Connecticut, North Carolina and Puerto Rico. A new world-wide association, Individualizing Instruction and Learning, located in Provo, Utah, has also begun to schedule workshops in this area.

Nongraded Expertise Seminars

On the other side of the coin, it will be extremely useful to invite nongraded consultants to the school so that teachers may have the benefit of their advice prior to taking actual steps. The daily fee for expertise such as this usually runs as high as $500 per day. Obviously, unless the district is very affluent, it is good economic practice to make full use of the advice which can be rendered by the expert in such areas as group procedures, reporting to parents, public information, and any and all other questionable items relevant to initiating a successful nongraded program. If possible, it is recommended that one session be scheduled during which the expert may speak to teachers and parents. This is usually more effective than if the local school administrators or faculty handled all the presentations with reference to the concept. Besides the fact that a new face and the "expert" title is always exciting, he is probably more generally knowledgeable and, consequently, able to draw upon an accumulation of practices and procedures from past experiences.

Nongraded Bulletin

There should be special publications on nongraded education emanating from the school. A monthly nongraded newsletter should be regularly sent out to parents and teachers informing them about the progress being made prior to the inception of the program and during its implementation. A sample of this is illustrated in Appendix A. In addition, a Teacher Handbook should be compiled containing "do's" and "don'ts" relative to the nongraded program.

Teacher Understanding and Involvement

In the interests of initiating a nongraded program, once an administrator has made an attempt to orient a teacher to the nongraded philosophy, there should be ample opportunity for the teaching staff to come to their own decision about whether the nongraded program should be implemented in the school. It is important to bear in mind that without teacher involvement, without understanding of the concept by the teacher, and without a firm belief that the nongraded program will be an improvement over the educational program currently offered in the school district, the nongraded program is bound to fail. If the administrator performs his job of orientation well, there is little doubt that teachers will decide affirmatively with regard to adopting the nongraded program. The orientation could possibly extend over a period of six months to a year, or even two years. There is an especial need, if the majority of teachers are not unequivocally supportive of the nongraded concept, to implement the concept in a series of stages. In one school this was done by a series of Professional Conference Days to which experts were invited to speak and at which workshops were held which dealt with the various aspects of nongrading. Following these conference days, when teachers displayed eagerness to implement the nongraded program, pilot projects were assigned to the nongraded program and various elements of planning were entered into and discussed by the elementary principal and teachers. Next, support of teachers and parents for the pilot program was elicited. During this period, nongraded bulletins were sent home to orient parents to the concept of the nongraded philosophy. Eventually, a number of parents attended a regular board meeting and voiced their support of the nongraded program. However, the author would stress that this procedure is extremely delicate and should be undertaken with care, particularly if there is any sensitivity among board members who might feel that the principal used subversive tactics to gain support of community residents for his innovative educational goals. A sample of a circular used to involve parents in plans for adoption of a nongraded educational program is illustrated in Appendix B. At this particular meeting, an excellent example of the kind of emotions which can be aroused in these circumstances occurred when a board member accused the principal of "shoving the nongraded principle down his throat." Fortunately for the principal, he had strong parental support which did not waiver and, as a result of the confrontation between these parents and the board of education, the board approved the adoption of the nongraded concept. The next step is for the principal, with the aid of a nongraded team composed of every teacher who would be involved in implementing the pilot project, to hold meetings and conferences to devise a handbook on the nongraded concept which is to be sent home to parents explaining the transformation from graded to nongraded. An example of such a handbook is illustrated in Appendix C.

During the first year there should be complete involvement on the part of all teachers affected by the program. The following technique has been used successfully:

School was cancelled for an entire day. During the morning session of this day, a professor from a nearby university visited the school and spoke about the humanistic transformation of education. After his presentation, teachers were asked to form groups and submit their recommendations for the solution of a number of problems involved in the implementation of the program. A sample of the program used for this day is illustrated in Appendix D. Teachers then met in groups and elected their spokesman, who was to be responsible for voicing their joint recommendations and suggestions in connection with the initiation of the program. In addition to this, all teachers met throughout the school year in their respective groups and voiced further recommendations. Utilizing the teachers' recommendations, the principal then devised a Preliminary Nongraded Implementation Plan, as illustrated in Appendix E. The plan was then submitted to all teachers for their reactions and the addition of substance to the preliminary plan. This technique was highly effective and gained ample teacher involvement so that the implementation of the program was accomplished smoothly. The foregoing procedure is not offered as a panacea, but as an indication of one successful method, and of the need for careful planning and consideration.

Timetable for Initiating the Nongraded Program

The author suggests the chart illustrated in Figure 4-1, on page 75 as a timetable for initiating the nongraded program within a period of one year prior to inception of the program.

Collection of nongraded materials is scheduled only for a five-month period beginning in September. It is also suggested that the summer months be utilized for preparation of requests to be forwarded to various school districts throughout the country in connection with information and/or materials.

Visits to nongraded schools are scheduled to begin in October. The basic reason for this is to allow teachers the month of September to arrange their own classrooms before visiting outside classrooms. Additionally, the school to be visited often needs the month of September to assist students and make necessary preparations to receive visitors in their classrooms. Needless to say, it is incumbent that visitations always be preceded by advance notice.

Nongraded workshops are scheduled to begin during the month of February, after all of the other activities have been initiated. These workshops are scheduled throughout the summer months. One of the reasons for scheduling the workshops during February is to provide ample time for administrators and teachers to make their

Actions	Sept.	Oct.	Nov.	Dec.	Jan.	Feb.	Mar.	Apr.	May	June	July
Collecting Nongraded Materials	x	x	x	x	x						
Visiting Nongraded Schools		x	x	x	x	x	x	x	x	x	
Conducting Nongraded Workshops						x	x	x	x	x	x
Publishing Nongraded Bulletins		x	x	x	x	x	x	x	x	x	x
Organizing Nongraded Expertise Seminars		x		x		x	x	x	x	x	x
Obtaining Teacher Under-standing and Involvement	x	x	x	x	x	x	x	x	x	x	x

Figure 4-1. *Timetable for initiating the nongraded program.*

selection from among the experts available of that person, or persons, they consider most suitable to conduct the workshops.

The nongraded expertise seminars are not to be conducted during the month of September primarily for the same reason that nongraded visits are not made during this month — to allow teachers the necessary time to attend to their students, arrange their classrooms, set up schedules, etc. During the balance of the year, consultants should be invited in every other month up to the second half of the school term. These limitations are invoked primarily because of the cost factor involved. However, if the particular school can afford the expense of year-round nongraded expertise, it is all to the better. Otherwise, the periodic visits by experts up to February (the time when the seminars begin and the workshops end) will be quite sufficient.

Nongraded bulletins should be transmitted to parents in October informing them of some aspects of nongraded education. Monthly, a special bulletin should be sent to all professional employees, elaborating on certain technical aspects of nongradedness and containing a progress report on the school's nongraded program.

Teacher understanding and involvement is essential and should be maintained for the entire school year.

Teacher and Parent Involvement

The most important element to be remembered when initiating the nongraded program is the necessity for teacher involvement. Teachers must be active participants in all phases of the nongraded program if it is to succeed. However, the fact still remains that teacher involvement alone is not sufficient to initiate a successful nongraded program. The program must be meticulously planned in collaboration with teachers and parents. Because the author was cognizant of this most vital aspect when initiating the nongraded program in his own school district, funds were requested from Title I, ESEA, to enable parents and teachers to visit a number of nongraded schools around the country. These trips were a huge success, not only because many of the teachers and parents had had little opportunity to travel, but also because they felt an intimate involvement in the plans and decisions of the school district. Painstaking care was exercised, however, to choose only those schools for visitation which best exemplified nongraded practices. These visitations were so effective that, upon their return, parents demanded that the Board of Education and the administration make the nongraded school a reality in their school district. The trips also served the ever-present need of bettering school-community relations, since teachers served as informative sources for parents and both were able to communicate with each other in a somewhat more relaxed atmosphere.

Specific Guidelines on the Successful Transition from Traditional Education to Nongraded Education

1. Read everything which is labeled "nongraded" and "individualized instruction." starting with Drs. John I. Goodlad and Robert H. Anderson's classic work.[1]

2. Visit as many nongraded schools as possible, traveling both locally and nationwide. Federal funds can be obtained for these traveling expenses under ESEA, Title I. Even if the schools are not really nongraded, there is always something of value which may be learned and taken into consideration.

3. Create a library center on nongraded materials, books, articles, recordings and films. Some films and recordings can be obtained, respectively, from the University of California in Los Angeles and the National Education Association.

4. When a school visited is found to be an exemplary model of nongraded organization and practice, if it is at all possible, parents, board members and teachers should be allowed to visit the school (or schools) so that they may have a personal view of the nongraded concept in practice.

5. Attend all nongraded seminars and conferences. Unfortunately, most universities and teacher training institutions do not offer formal courses in nongraded principles at present. If they should do so in the future, attendance at these classes is highly recommended.

6. It is important that discussions be had with as many people as possible in connection with their ideas about the

---

[1] John I. Goodlad and Robert H. Anderson, The Nongraded Elementary School (Harcourt, Brace & World, Inc., New York, 1963).

nongraded concept. These might include principals, students, teachers and experts on the nongraded philosophy. In one school district a Speakerphone was installed and a call placed to Dr. Anderson at Harvard University. During this conversation, professional staff members had the opportunity to speak directly to Dr. Anderson, addressing queries that had arisen and receiving his immediate response.

In point of time, it will take administrators and teachers at least a year to become thoroughly familiar with all aspects of the nongraded concept. Therefore, do not expect to be able to answer all questions which may be posed by board members, parents and teachers until ample indoctrination in the nongraded concept has taken place.

7. Teachers should be asked to serve voluntarily on nongraded committees. The primary function of a nongraded committee is to keep teachers informed of current developments, to recommend and make visits to nongraded schools, to conduct research in certain problem areas, and to make certain tentative decisions prior to discussion with the entire professional staff.

8. Where teachers are not thoroughly convinced about the usefulness of the nongraded concept, it is preferable to proceed slowly in its implementation, correlating adoption of the program to the amount of teacher support for it. Eventually, most of these teachers will "bootleg" the nongraded concept and there will be no necessity to continue selling them on the philosophy, for they will begin to sell themselves. In one particular school district, an administrator was picketed when the nongraded concept was first implemented at the latter part of a school year. When some two months had elapsed, the teacher most vociferous during the picketing appeared before the administrator with apologies and a request that the entire school be nongraded.

9. Nongraded newsletters should be circulated regularly to keep staff and parents informed of all current developments.

10. Some parents are not receptive to change. It may be necessary for an administrator who is contemplating the transition to nongradedness to implement the nongraded program on a partial basis at the beginning. If all steps have been taken to insure the efficiency of the nongraded plan, most parents will soon demand themselves that the entire school become nongraded.

11. Obtain the board of education's sanction to the program. In this connection, community support for the program has often served as an agent of persuasion to many boards of education.

12. Provide orientation for students in the nongraded program. Willingness on the part of students, as well as teachers, to be involved in the new program is a direct result of properly introducing them to its concepts.

13. The success or failure of the nongraded program rests on how well it has been organizationally structured. The staff must undertake detailed planning on how to individualize instruction. All of the most exemplary nongraded schools are well organized, with specific procedures for the individualization of instruction.

14. Determine if there are adequate supplies, materials, equipment, and furniture to effectuate the nongraded program, and provide for their acquisition, if necessary.

15. A decision should be made, in collaboration with the professional staff, as to whether only one subject area or the entire school program will be nongraded. Only then should steps be undertaken to prepare the nongraded curriculum, which is one of the most integral parts of the nongraded program, and can signal its success or failure.

SUMMARY

It is extremely important that administrators and staff members of the school make careful plans to achieve an effective plan for initiating the nongraded program. In order to accomplish this purpose, intimate involvement by administrators, teachers, students, and parents, is crucial. Among other things, there must be an ample collection of nongraded materials for review; parents should be afforded every opportunity to visit nongraded classes at various schools; and staff members should be exposed to workshops, seminars and lectures in order that they may not only provide resources in building the program but also that they may be better able to maintain the program effectively. Administrators should make every attempt to invite numerous experts to the school, and circulate nongraded bulletins which provide regular periodic information to parents to keep them abreast of all developments in the program. Above all else, these efforts should be undertaken with that most important person, the student, in mind.

5. DESCRIPTION OF THREE NONGRADED CURRICULUM PLANS

The curriculum is the heart of a school's program.

Robert H. Anderson

Although the key to the successful implementation of the nongraded program rests with teachers, their abilities, and their attitudes toward rejecting the traditional approach to educating children, in favor of accepting and implementing the concept of individualization of instruction, the curriculum is almost equally important. Careful consideration must be given to the question of how the nongraded curriculum is to be employed in the instructional program, for without an organized curriculum to meet individualized instructional needs, the implementation of an adequate nongraded plan is impossible. Therefore, a number of plans will be described herein for the educator's final determination of which plan or combination of plans will best suit the needs of his student population within the limits of his educational faculty and facilities. The nongraded curriculum must be designed so as to encompass certain basic and fundamental characteristics, among them the following:

1. It must be individual-child oriented; that is, the curriculum must be directed to meet the abilities, needs, and interests of each individual child.

2. It must be experience-oriented in order to present the child with daily realities so that his day-to-day learning is relevant and meaningful to him.

3. It must be socially oriented and directed toward the society in which the child lives, for he is a part of that society.

4. It must be community-oriented so that it will prepare and assist the student in his understanding of and adjustment to the activities, needs, and resources of his community.

As an analogy, the nongraded curriculum might be compared to several large circles placed together so that each circle overlaps another, with the individual child standing at the core of the circles. In this picture, if a single circle is omitted, serious deficiency in the curriculum will result.

There are generally three basic nongraded curriculum plans or formats. A single one or a combination of two or three may be implemented in the initiation of a nongraded program, dependent upon the characteristics of the school involved.

Skill or Concept Sequence Plan

This plan usually is built around the subject areas of reading, mathematics and the language arts, for the reason that these areas are heavily involved with the development of skills which may be easily related to other areas, and are indeed necessary to success in other areas. The Concept Sequence Plan usually takes in the areas of social studies and science although, at times, there are certain skills which must be acquired in conjunction with the concepts. For example, in science, a skill could very well be learning the operation of a microscope and in social studies, a related skill could be learning how to read a map.

The Skill Sequence Plan is probably the most simple and expeditious method of organizing the curriculum to accommodate a nongraded program, and it is readily apparent that many school districts consider these factors in devising this curriculum plan. John L. Tewksbury substantiates this in his book, when he recommends:

"In arithmetic, each book could consist of a section of the basal text or workbook. Each book could be divided into five to eight sections. From a child's standpoint, there would appear to be advantages in having the book divided into sections (levels), each of which would take only part of the school year to complete. Many children can work better on goals which are closer than those which are far removed in time. The staff of a school would decide which chapters to include in each level."[1]

At this point, it seems appropriate to discuss the identifying connotation of "level" as opposed to "grade." The essential difference is that a level represents a given number of basic skills, mastery of which is designated to be accomplished within a specific allotment of time.

However, some administrators have utilized this plan in a manner which serves merely to substitute level sequence for grade sequence which, in many cases, accounts for the failure of so many schools to successfully implement a true nongraded program. In other words, they must devise materials for skills as opposed to grades. At present, if a parent is told that his child is in third grade, he actually has no idea about the real achievement level of his child, since there is a very wide range of achievement among pupils assigned to third grade. The use of skill levels provides meaningful knowledge to parents with regard to the child's particular competencies, as opposed to the vagueness of reference to a meaningless, but traditional, second, third or fourth grade. An example of a partial outline of content and expectations in skill subjects such as language arts and arithmetic is illustrated:

LEVEL I

Language Arts

1. Mastery of proper nouns in the first basic pre-primer
2. An awareness of rhyming words
3. An awareness of beginning sounds
4. Recognition of color words
5. Language development through vocabulary enrichment by organizing thoughts into sentences (orally)

---

[1] John L. Tewksbury, *Nongrading in the Elementary School* (Charles E. Merrill Publishing Company, 1300 Alum Creek Drive, Columbus, Ohio, 1967), p. 44. Reprinted with permission.

6. Eye-hand coordination
7. Left to right reading of pictures

LEVEL II

Language Arts

1. Mastery of the vocabulary of the basic pre-primer reading text
2. Knowledge of color words and number words
3. Printing name legibly
4. Forming letters correctly with direction
5. Picture reading – ability to get meaning from a picture
6. Phonics – auditory recognition of beginning sounds

LEVEL I

Arithmetic

1. Set theory and cardinal numbers 1-5
2. Counting 1-10
3. Recognizing symbols 1-10
4. Number concepts to 10
5. Denominate numbers
   a. Calendar and clock – introduce days, weeks, hours, and minutes
6. Matching shapes
7. Understanding comparison terms – smaller, larger, more, less
8. Ordinals – 1st - 5th
9. Points and line

LEVEL II

Arithmetic

1. Set theory and number concepts 1-10
2. Understanding the writing of numbers, etc.
3. Denominate numbers
   a. Calendar – days, weeks
   b. Money – penny, nickel, dime
4. Addition and subtraction combinations through 6
5. Recognizing and naming shapes
6. Addition – concept of adding one more
7. Ordinals – 1st through 10th

The level sequence plan is most frequently used in elementary schools. This permits each student to progress from one level to another as rapidly as he can master the skills and content. After the child has demonstrated his competency at a given level, a skill mastery test is administered and, if he maintains 85 percent correct responses, he then proceeds to another level. In those cases where mastery or completion of the skill level is not successfully achieved, new materials are provided for the student which will aid him in conquering the specific weakness which prevents his acquisition of the skill. When it is felt that these materials have served the purpose for which they were designed, the child is then retested for mastery of the skill with a new examination.

Among the numerous advantages of utilizing the Skill or Concept Sequence Plan are the following:

1. Such plan is easy to construct. Preparation of content involves the simple excerption of desired information from the body of a series of textbooks;

2. Adequate records can be easily kept for the purpose of recording individual programs of students;

3. Adequate provision can be made for sequential steps in the acquisition of basic skills;

4. Individualized achievement is facilitated so that when a child completes a level, he may go on to the next level without affecting his classmates' rate of progress. In other words, it permits each child to advance through the required curriculum according to his potential, at his own rate of progress;

5. There is opportunity to administer frequent, periodic tests which provide timely evaluation of how much a student has mastered and identification of weak areas requiring greater concentration, alleviating the nonproductive "plodding along" until a final examination uncovers a weakness which might have been corrected earlier had it been known.

However, the foregoing advantages must be considered in conjunction with the following disadvantages in order to assess the true value of this plan:

1. A constant vigil must be kept to assure that teachers do not succumb to the tendency to equate skill levels with grade levels;

2. Effectiveness of the plan is relative to and highly dependent upon utilization of various educational materials, tools, and equipment to accommodate the curriculum;

3. Content is usually limited;

4. There is an ever-present danger of regression to the traditional curriculum guide;

5. Too often, there is the demand that each level must be mastered before procedure to the next level is permitted;

6. Painstaking care must be taken to assure that flexibility is built into the curriculum;

7. Content is often narrow and nondescriptive.

Individual Study Unit Plan

These units are sometimes referred to as a "Learning Activity Package," or "Unipac," or "Teaching-Learning Units," or as "Concept Centered Courses" or "Contracts" or "Computer Instruction Units." Regardless of the descriptive title used, all of these fall into the category of Individual Study Units. The guiding principle underlying individual study units is to provide each child with a curriculum so that he is assured of an individualized instructional program. This plan is found in elementary and secondary schools. An individual study unit in social studies might deal with transportation concepts—what transportation is, the basic types of transportation, the development of transportation through the ages as cultural needs changed, and the socio-cultural and economic significance of transportation in terms of modern usage. The package would include tests to determine weak and strong points among students in the area; and a text and slides to illustrate sub-concepts which, with teacher guidance, will familiarize the student with the stated concepts so that he may accomplish the behavioral objective of presenting a composite picture of transportation from the early ages through modern times.

Learning Activity Packages

The Nova School in Fort Lauderdale, Florida is well known for the use of Learning Activity Packages which constitute the core of their program. Each teacher on the Nova staff is assigned to a subject area program in which LAP's are to be developed. The following steps are usually taken in the development of LAP's:

1. The teacher develops the scope and sequence for the particular area or subject which he is involved in writing.

2. A pre-test may or may not be included with the LAP. The purpose of the pre-test is to determine what and how much the student already knows about the subject area. This pre-test will also indicate where student strengths and weaknesses may lie in the particular area for which a LAP is to be prescribed.

3. The teacher then lists in serial order the concepts which are to be covered in the entire sequence of LAP's for the particular subject area.

4. If there are accompanying sub-concepts which a student should be exposed to, then they should be listed also for presentation in the LAP's.

5. A descriptive title should be assigned to the LAP referring to the subject area covered, such as "Exploring Contemporary Physics" or "Critical Thinking in Mathematics."

6. Behavioral objectives or goals should be listed initially so that they may later be used as measuring devices to determine what has or has not been learned.

7. Behavioral objectives or goals should be analyzed to insure that they are relevant to the concepts, and that they are couched in measurable terms.

8. A list should be prepared containing all assignments or activities which students are to follow in order to reach the goals forecast by the LAP's. In preparing this section of the LAP, the teacher should consider a variety of grouping procedures, several textbooks, and a multitude of educational technology and other materials.

9. The teacher should then recheck those materials to be included in the LAP to ascertain that the assignments and activities are pertinent to meeting the stated behavioral goals and objectives.

10. A self-evaluation test should be prepared to enable students to test themselves whenever they feel they are ready to take the post or final test.

11. A final or post-test should be prepared to be given to those students who feel they are ready for it. When and if the student passes this test, he is directed to the next LAP in the particular subject area series. If he maintains a certain number of correct responses, he should then be re-cycled through the activities of the LAP.

An outline of a sample unit, described in the contents of a Learning Activities Package in transportation at the Nova School in Fort Lauderdale, Florida, is as follows:

Table of Contents*

----

*Reprinted by permission.

Contracts

The contract format for individual study units has been used with remarkable success in the public schools of Duluth, Minnesota. This method involves the preparation of a "contract" to achieve certain specific instructional objectives in the particular unit of a subject area to be studied. As may be seen by the illustration on the following page of a contract in Geography used by the Duluth Public Schools, six instructional objectives should be covered in the contract: Content Classification, Purpose, Criterion Performance, Sample Test Situation, Taxonomy Category and Resources. In view of the broad range of intellectual activities it is important to carefully identify the taxonomy category which most nearly fits the instructional objective. Among the categories which might fall under consideration are knowledge, comprehension, application, analysis, synthesis, invention or evaluation, but the Duluth Public Schools have used a classification scheme employing only four categories, i.e., knowledge, comprehension, application and invention.

Computer Instructional Units

Some school districts have elected to utilize Computer Instructional Units. A group of teachers acting together in a workshop setting designate a particular unit of work in a particular subject area for which they will develop computer resource units specifying the objectives, content, activities, materials and measuring devices which are to be related to learner characteristics. The variables, or learner characteristics, which have been predetermined by a series of diagnostic tests for the purpose, are then coded for utilization into each computer work unit in terms of intelligence

Contract Used in the Duluth Public Schools*

Name _____

Date issued _____

Date due _____

53-2

CONTENT CLASSIFICATION
  I. Geography of the United States
      A. Major River Systems and Water Bodies

PURPOSE
  To help the student become familiar with these major water formations in preparation for future study.

CRITERION PERFORMANCE
  Given a map of the United States, the student will be able to identify all major river systems and lakes with 90% accuracy.

SAMPLE TEST SITUATION

A. _____

B. _____

C. _____

D. _____

TAXONOMY CATEGORY
  Knowledge

RESOURCES
____ A. The South - Fideler, p. 33

____ B. California and The West - Fideler, p. 242-250.

____ C. The Midwest - Fideler, p. 77

____ D. Great Plains States - Fideler, p. 9

____ E. all related games and flashcards

____ F. Ginn World Atlas and workbook

Figure 5-1

_____

*Reprinted by permission of The Board of Education of the City of Duluth, Minnesota.

quotient, sex, grade level, reading level, child's interests, vital statistics, social class, handicapped behavior, etc. Professional variables, such as major social functions, group activity, objectives, instructional materials, instructional activities, and evaluation devices are also fully developed in the resource guide. Each computer unit or work, therefore, has two components, the Resource Guide for Teachers and the Resource Guide for Pupils. The Teachers' Guide is arranged in sections, such as "Teaching Objectives," "Content Outlines," "Large Group Activities," "Small Group Activities," "Instructional Materials" and "Evaluation Devices." Using as an example the topical unit of transportation in social studies, one of the teaching objectives might be entitled "The Role of Transportation in the World Today," in which the content outline would include a cross-cultural analysis of goods transportation, seasonal effects on navigation in varied climates, and the effect of modern transportation activities on business. The objectives would be reached through large group activity such as field trips to transportation hubs; supportive instructional materials such as filmstrips and texts; and finally, an evaluation mechanism. The evaluation mechanism would include a pre-test and a post-test to determine whether objectives have been reached. These tests would be administered in conjunction with an instructor-prepared test to uncover factual knowledge amassed. The Resource Guide for Pupils with a print-out sheet, complementing the Teaching Objectives in the Resource Guide for Teachers, includes individual activities and individual instructional materials prescribed for the pupil according to his characteristics as encoded on an IBM card. Therefore, there may or may not be a prescription for individual activities for each objective for all pupils. Among the instructional activities is the preparation of comprehensive charts and reports, which, supported by a variety of texts, serve as individual instructional resource materials in the completion of individual activities.

The following is a report submitted by a team of mathematics teachers who visited Project Plan, a computer program being offered in the Hicksville School District, in Hicksville, Long Island:

> The Hicksville School System and 12 other schools throughout the United States were chosen to be involved in an experimental computer education program funded by a grant from Westinghouse.

The basic idea of the program was to provide an individualized curriculum for each student so that each student might best progress at his own rate of speed, in individual ability and achievement level. The computer was used as an administrative tool to keep records on each student, and to evaluate and prescribe for each student.

Teachers were trained for 8 months and given the opportunity to decide the basic objectives to be learned in each area, at each level. They then wrote multi-curricula designed to teach these basic skills and concepts on an individualized and small group basis.

Initially, diagnostic test results were programmed into the computer. The computer then determined at which areas or levels the individual student commenced learning. At frequent intervals, student progress was tested. The results were fed into the computer which "graded" the tests and indicated areas of weakness where the student had either failed to meet specific learning objectives, or was progressing at an expected pace. The computer, in addition to prescribing remedial procedures based upon a stored history, also determined future learning objectives, and the potential rate of progress for the individual student. Neither the teacher nor the student required a prior knowledge of computer operations or programming.

The curriculum incorporated a diverse number of audio-visual aids and manipulative devices. The teachers, trained at Palo Alto, California, spent the majority of their time in writing curriculum. They had access to a large variety of the aforementioned aids and, in addition, contacted many experts in the educational field. All expertise, literature and devices were applied to curriculum development, or "Teacher Learning Units."

Elementary School

We observed the first and fifth grades. There were two classes of 25 students in the first grade combined into one class with two teachers cooperating. As in the high school, these were set aside for each of the disciplines. Pupils received individual instruction form sheets called TLU's (Teacher Learning Units). Instructions for the students were in pictorial rather than written form. We were told that at this time there were only three curricula for each unit, while in the high school there were eight. All students seemed to be working, many operating tape recorders and record players with ear plugs. We were quite impressed by the excellent atmosphere in the room.

Every child seemed to know exactly what he or she was doing. Teachers were constantly working with small groups. A chart to track the progress of each student was on the back wall. However, we felt that this might have had an adverse effect on the slower students. Teachers seemed to work harder in this program than in the familiar, traditional set-up. The principal seemed to feel that much of the success of this program was due to the two particular teachers assigned to it. In our opinion, the computer was not optimally used, and we felt that the teacher's role might be greatly eased were the computer role increased.

The fifth grade students were following the same procedure. They used two connecting rooms for two classes, each with 30 students. One room was used for Science and Math, while the other was being used for English and Social Studies. There seemed to be a little confusion and some inattention at this level, but the total atmosphere was still good. Most students went about their work with little or no supervision. Teachers worked with small groups. Teachers at this level seemed to have more difficulty adjusting to this new role than the first grade teachers.

We were told that, at present, there are second and sixth grade teachers being trained and writing curricula. These teachers were away until June. Curricula are constantly re-evaluated and modified or rewritten.

Junior High

Ninety students are involved on the ninth grade level. Students seem to be well-motivated and working well, both individually and in small groups of twos and threes. The rooms had a variety of audio-visual equipment as well as many reference books. These students did not use texts per se but rather the audio-visual aids and reference materials. We noticed that although a greater variety of equipment and books was available, less of each type was needed, since few students were at the same point at any precise time. We also noticed that the teacher's role changed from the traditional lecturer and discussion leader to advisor and reference person. This new role caused difficulties for at least one of the four teachers involved, and we foresee the possibility of a major problem in this respect. Most motivation was intrinsic to the material used. In some cases, where problems did arise, the student involved entered into a written contract with the teacher which allowed the student to follow whatever courses he wanted for a specific period if he finished a particular number of prescribed units first. The teachers seemed to feel that this was a successful technique. Although this project was on different grade levels, we saw it as the beginning of an ungraded situation where all students could work at their own levels, as indicated by their own ability, and progress at an individualized rate. One obvious drawback to this particular program was the marking system. Teachers were told by the school administration to give a numerical grade. This is virtually impossible, but, nevertheless, is being complied with.

For educators who are interested in visiting those school districts now exploring the use of computerized instructional units, the following list may serve as a guide:

Bethel Park School District
Bethel Park, Pennsylvania

Hicksville Public School District
Hicksville, Long Island, New York

Pittsburgh Public Schools
Pittsburgh, Pennsylvania

Quincy Public Schools
Quincy, Massachusetts

Wood County Schools
Parkersburg, West Virginia

Archdiocese of San Francisco
San Francisco, California

Fremont Unified School District
Fremont, California

San Carlos Elementary School District
San Carlos, California

San Jose City Unified School District
San Jose, California

Sequoia Union High School District
Redwood City, California

Union Elementary School District
San Jose, California

Penn-Trafford School District
Harrison City, Pennsylvania

Santa Clara Unified School District
Santa Clara, California
Hughson Union High School District
Hughson, California

The advantages of the Individual Study Unit Plan, some of which are immediately recognizable, consist of:

1. It is an immediately individualized approach to education.
2. Careful planning of this curriculum will assure the satisfaction of individual needs.
3. The pressure of time limitation is removed, so that students are afforded the means of completing their own individual study units according to the boundaries set by their own abilities and interests, sometimes acquiring skills and learning concepts simultaneously.
4. There is an explicitness in direction that can easily be adhered to.
5. The plan is comprehensive in scope. The Individual Study Unit Plan provides opportunities for individualization while, at the same time, providing opportunities for socialization.

Among the disadvantages of implementing this plan are:

1. An extended period of time in which to devise the plan is required.
2. Potentially prohibitive expense might be incurred in terms of relieving teachers to prepare the units.
3. In some schools, insofar as the Computer Instructional Units are concerned, the program does not allow for the socialization aspect which is an important element of the educational program.
4. The expenditure for the computer unit might be prohibitive for certain school districts.
5. There is a lack of sequential steps.

The Multiple Phase Plan

This plan is implemented by most nongraded high schools, with certain deviations. Actually, it originated in 1958 with the establishment of the first nongraded school in Melbourne, Florida; and similar plans have since been utilized in other nongraded schools, among them: Wheatland Chili School in Scottsville, New York; the Elridge School in Elridge, Illinois; and the Amherst Regional High School in Amherst, Massachusetts. In the Multiple Phase Plan, a large amount of attention must be directed toward all factors influencing the student's choice of electives and phase levels. Particularly in the selection of electives, teachers, guidance counselors and parents should serve as sources of consultation for the student seeking to define his particular interest and set realistic goals for himself. The ultimate determining factor in course selection will, of course, lie with the desires of parent and student but there is allowance, during reviews each spring, for future revisions in the tentative four-year program chosen, predicated upon subsequent achievement in the program and/or an alteration in goals. Phase or Achievement Levels selected by the student lay further emphasis on individualization by permitting the student to gear his needs, interests and achievement probabilities to his program of study in each subject area. For example, a student might choose Phase I in mathematics, which is a course designed for students needing special assistance, and stresses remediation, special individual attention and aid in surmounting individual learning problems. The same student might choose Phase 4 in social studies, which is designed for students seeking exploration in depth of a particular subject and who can, therefore, be expected to have good command of basic, required, and relevant skills to accomplish the major part of achievement through independent efforts with little teacher assistance. Illustrated below are the prerequisites, description, and content of various suggested phase levels. It is important to bear in mind that phases are indicative of achievement levels only, and do not represent intelligence levels. Consequently, a student might be rephased at any time it is considered feasible. Also illustrated is a description of the partial Multi-Phase Program in United States History offered by the Amherst Regional High School in Amherst, Massachusetts:

Achievement Level Grouping*

In keeping with our philosophy of individualizing our educational program, a student will ordinarily be permitted to

---

*Reprinted by permission.

select a particular achievement level in each of his courses. The achievement levels or phases represent an attempt to match our program to the needs, interests, and achievement of each pupil without reference to his grade level placement. The following phases are listed for your reference:

Phase   *Description*

1. Designed for students needing special assistance.
2. Designed for students needing an emphasis on basic skills.
3. Designed for students with an average background of achievement.
4. Designed for exploration in depth.
5. Designed for students with a superior background of achievement and self-motivation.
Q The "Quest" Phase – independent study
X Unphased courses

Phase 1

The student who selects the achievement level of Phase 1 in a particular course has identified himself as a remedial student in that subject area. Through this selection he has shown his need for special individual attention and assistance in demonstrating his learning activities.

The student in a Phase 1 class will be expected to:

1. attend all assigned classes regularly;
2. complete all assignments, and hand in class work on time;
3. be willing to participate in some class discussion;
4. read or work in class with all assigned materials under teacher supervision and guidance;
5. demonstrate a positive attitude by attempting individual projects and requesting special assistance when needed;
6. practice the several skills required in each subject (speaking, writing, etc.)

Phase 2

The student who selects the achievement level of Phase 2 in a particular course will be expected to show achievement beyond the remedial and special assistance level. The student will receive much direction and assistance from the teacher in the classroom.

The student in a Phase 2 class will be expected to:

1. attend all assigned classes regularly;
2. complete all assignments and hand in class assignments on time;

3. be willing to participate in class discussion especially relating to his own personal experiences to the subject;
4. read or work with all assigned materials under teacher direction and supervision;
5. learn to develop reading skills, write short sentences, spell correctly, and communicate properly;
6. demonstrate tolerance by giving and taking positive criticism from teachers and fellow students;
7. demonstrate positive attitudes by attempting individual projects and working in harmony with other members of the class;
8. demonstrate the several skills required in each class with limited practice.

Phase 3

The student who selects the achievement level of Phase 3 in a particular course should be able to use concrete information in generalizations and abstractions and do this with limited teacher direction. In this phase, the student will be expected to demonstrate some other learning activities independent of teacher supervision.

The student in Phase 3 class will be expected to:

1. attend all assigned classes regularly;
2. be able to read or work with all assigned materials without special assistance from the teacher;
3. complete a limited number of assignments outside of the class;
4. be able to use libraries and other resource centers with limited teacher direction;
5. participate in frequent and analytical class discussion;
6. employ inductive as well as deductive reasoning in class participation and individual projects;
7. demonstrate several skills required in each class;
8. be conscientious in completing assignments and handling both in-class and out-of-class work.

Phase 4

The student who selects the achievement level of Phase 4 in a particular course should expect to demonstrate a major part of his achievement without teacher assistance. In choosing this high achievement phase the student indicates that he has a command of the basic skills required in that subject matter field.

The student in a Phase 4 class will be expected to:

1. read or work in considerable depth with all materials and experiment with related materials;
2. demonstrate an independence in developing conclusions, interpreting information, and employing insight and original thought through oral and written expression;
3. prepare in advance of class discussions a comprehensive investigation of the topics of discussion, and a documented organization of material;
4. employ a considerable amount of inductive as well as deductive reasoning in the analysis of problems;
5. be willing to devote a large portion of time and energy to independent research in the library and other resource centers;
6. complete different types of activities that will demonstrate quality of achievement in learning.

Phase 5

The student who selects the achievement level of Phase 5 in a particular course has designated his achievement level to be beyond the basic perception level. It is assumed that the student has extended his conceptual development into analytical and creative thinking. The student entering a Phase 5 course will be expected to cultivate a mature expression of his abilities, learnings, and feelings. In relation to that subject matter field in which he chooses this achievement level, the student should know:

A. Certain related terminology
B. Trends and sequences
C. Criteria for testing facts, principles, and opinions
D. Principles and generalizations
E. Theories and structures.

The student in a Phase 5 course will be expected to:

1. have developed or expressed a sincere interest in the particular field or knowledge related to the course which he selects
2. undertake work of considerable depth and variety
3. assume a major portion of the responsibility for his own achievement
4. demonstrate a sophistication in the expression of original thought and critical analysis
5. prepare a number of independent projects through use of the library and other resource centers
6. demonstrate creative as well as expository abilities by the preparation and presentation of extensive research studies

7. pursue some part of the learning activities in the course on a completely independent basis
8. complete a college level program of studies (in some Phase 5 courses).

The Quest Phase deserves clarification. This is a rigorous program of independent study and research in depth initiated by a student who demonstrates qualities for such work and who, with the advice of a faculty consultant, expects to acquire more knowledge than students in a conventional class. The student must design a specific problem with the aid of a consulting teacher and must fulfill other requirements before he is admitted to the Quest Program.

Every attempt will be made to place a student in class sections according to his phase levels in particular subjects (not necessarily the same phase level in each subject), and the staff will be prepared to phase a student as an individual or as a member of a smaller group within a class section. Although school personnel recommend each phase placement, the students play the major role in selection of phases. Finally, since phases represent achievement levels, NOT INTELLIGENCE GROUPS, a student may be rephased at any time.

United States History

Phase 1

1. The Phase 1 United States History Course is designed to give the students a great deal of assistance in the development of certain basic skills, but other instruction such as the use of statistical information and the news media will be included.

2. The material used in this course will cover the chronological period 1865 through the present in United States History. Reading materials of a basic nature will be used in class.

3. The students should expect to use a considerable number of audio-visual materials, and to voluntarily engage in participatory projects, with emphasis in the social studies area.

4. Evaluation will be based primarily on each student's willingness, consistency, and punctuality of participation in class activities and projects.

Phase 2

1. Students entering this phase should have a limited, but workable ability to read from secondary and primary sources. Assistance in the development of this skill will be provided by the teacher through class work.

2. The Phase 2 student will be expected to achieve skills in reading maps and in gathering information from diagrams, graphs, pictures, and the news media. Audio-visual aids will play a major role in this development.

3. Evaluation will be partially based on the student's willingness and ability to participate in class discussions and projects. Almost all work will be done in class under the direct supervision of the teacher.

Phase 3

1. The Phase 3 student should be able to read the required text, which will be a major source of factual information. Chronologically, the course will cover the period 1865 through the present.

2. Students must expect to be tested on their understanding of and their ability to remember the factual material from the various readings.

3. The Phase 3 student will also be evaluated on the basis of his willingness and ability to express his conclusions in class and to present carefully written homework exercises.

4. Much emphasis will be placed on the development of skills common to the social studies -- reading, information gathering from various types of sources, and drawing conclusions.

Phase 4

1. The Phase 4 course will be oriented towards a topical approach to United States History. Units of study which examine problems common to the various chronological periods, from 1865 through the present, will be used. Such topics as civil liberties, immigration, foreign policy, economic depression, and political reform will be dealt with.

2. Emphasis will be placed upon the student's ability to read, to analyze the problems presented, to develop hypotheses, and to undertake research for historical substantiation.

3. Evaluation will be based in large part on the student's willingness and ability to contribute in a constructive way to the class discussion of the issues involved in the various topics.

4. During the year the students will be required to demonstrate their ability to use the skills of historical investigation and writing in the preparation of at least two research projects.

Phase 5

1. The student entering Phase 5 should be prepared to be responsible for a major portion of his own achievement.

The student should also understand that this work will make large demands upon his time and his energy.

2. To assist the students in preparing for the Advanced Placement Examination, the course will cover the chronological period 1492 through the present. The students will be expected to read and to remember much factual information, to be drawn from a variety of sources, both primary and secondary.

3. The Phase 5 student will also use materials, other than the highly factual, which will require him to interpret information, to draw conclusions, and to express himself both in written and in oral form.

4. The students will be required to undertake a number of projects designed to develop and to test their ability to use the proper historical methods of research, documentation, and writing.

The advantages of the Multiple Phase Plan are readily recognizable:

1. It offers more latitude than the Individual Study Units.

2. Students are permitted more freedom in the selection of what they are to learn.

3. Parents may become involved in the area of study the child is pursuing.

4. It is comprehensive and sequential in design.

Among the disadvantages are:

1. It is similar to tracking, with the exception that the students can move from one track to another.

2. It is time-consuming to plan and prepare, especially when it is borne in mind that a curriculum plan must be devised for each phase.

3. Students are soon identified by abilities.

4. The composition of the phases utilizes a structure which includes traditional labels such as "average background" and "superior achievement."

5. Lecturing to the student is a dominant feature in some schools instituting this plan.

6. Individuality is not always a part of classroom activity.

Budget Implications for
Implementing the Nongraded Concept

No matter what anyone may say, the present traditional classroom is not sufficiently equipped with appropriate materials, equipment, furniture or supplies to effectively serve a nongraded program. In the past, traditional classrooms were organized and structured to deal with an entire class as a single unit. Nongraded education predicates treating each student as a single unit and it will, therefore, cost the taxpayer more money if the individualization is to be properly accomplished. The need for additional funds is obvious when the following needs are taken into account:

1. Visits to model schools and attendance at seminars and conferences;

2. The purchase of books and journals to accomplish the compilation of an extensive nongraded library;

3. Extra remuneration to, or release of, professional staff members to work on curriculum and in the latter case an allowance for substitutes' salaries;

4. Extensive duplication and reproduction of materials;

5. Honorariums to experts invited to speak to professional staff members and parents;

6. Purchase of additional furniture, supplies, books and equipment;

7. Structural renovations necessary to accommodate the many facets of individualized instruction;

8. Dissemination of nongraded materials; and

9. Remuneration for training and retention of teacher aides.

Cost for Curriculum Development

It is undoubtedly true that the greatest expense will lie in the area of curriculum development – and this is as it should be. The entire curriculum must be revised. Perhaps the most inexpensive method of curriculum revision is the Skilled Sequence Plan which is less time-consuming in its application. Next, in terms of least expense, is the Multiple Phase Plan because the acquisition of large equipment, such as computers, is not essential to curriculum adequacy. The most expensive of all the curriculum plans to institute is the Individual Study Unit Plan. The Nova School District, which utilizes the Learning Activity Packages, has spent more than several hundred thousands of dollars in their development.

Computer-assisted instruction is by far the most expensive because the professional staff members must devote full time to the development of computer instructional units. In addition, the cost of the computer alone is prohibitive to some school districts, varying in price range from $10,000 to several hundred thousand dollars.

All of this leads to the inevitable fact that taxpayers must be informed that if they want contemporary and improved education for their youngsters, they must be willing to pay for it. This is only too realistic in terms of increased technological advances, the transitional times and the concomitant increase in the cost of living, all of which support the painful, but necessary, increased educational expenses.

In some school districts, release planning for professional staff members engaged in curriculum revision is scheduled so that teachers perform normal school duties for only approximately 60 percent of the school day, and substitutes are called in to replace them for the balance of the day. It is possible through split-planning techniques to utilize only one substitute for two teachers by allowing release time for one teacher in the morning and, for the other, in the afternoon. Other school districts have preferred, where ample funds and competent substitute replacement personnel were available, to release professional staff members for the entire school year to work on development of curriculum. Both of these plans have some merit and the particular school district must decide which plan, or combination of the plans, will be most viable.

The Nongraded Concept in Higher Education

Although most of our colleges and universities frequently provide students with opportunities for individualized research projects, attendance at seminars, and small and large group instructional methods, most of them have not formalized their instructional procedures to fully incorporate the nongraded concept. In most cases, these universities expect all students taking a particular course to read the same text, take the same examinations and, for a portion of the course, to listen to the same lectures and see the same films or exhibits. In actuality, many graduate points are earned merely through students' attendance in class and preparation of a prescribed paper on the particular subject of the course.

Attempts have been made to informally introduce parts of the nongraded concept into the hallowed halls of institutions of higher education. Unfortunately, these attempts have been mere drops in a bucket which must be filled to overflowing for the benefit of young adults who have reached this stage in their education. Some colleges utilize advanced placement techniques which allow the high school student to take a comprehensive examination relating to material usually covered during the freshman year and, if the student does well on this test, he is allowed to skip this year. While many Ivy League colleges follow this practice, a number of other colleges, in particular the University of Chicago, allow advanced placement of several years of college according to scores obtained on tests. There are also many colleges which permit students to absent themselves from regular classes, view scheduled lessons on television and, upon successfully taking an examination, pass on to an advanced course. While all of these attempts to introduce certain aspects of the nongraded concept into higher education are to be commended, they are much too small in scope and far too isolated. Sooner or later, hopefully sooner, colleges and universities will realize the immense benefits which a humanistic, individualized approach can offer to their students, and the responsibility of higher institutions to provide extensive, specialized education. However, change is in the wind and this author believes it will not be too long before many colleges and universities will be following the splendid example set by Dr. Andrew McAllister, a brilliant educator who is President of East Coast University in Brooksville, Florida, which has been doing research in the field of individualized instruction for over twenty years. The example which East Coast University is setting has put pressure on colleges and universities across the nation, and there is no doubt that eventually they will imitate and expand on the program now offered by East Coast. One visiting East Coast University for the first time would not be favorably impressed with the physical plant. The institution is located in a large field and consists of two converted buildings which are used as centers for learning. Just as in the proverbial saying about judging a book by its cover, the exterior appearance of East Coast University bears no relation to the quality of its internalized capacity for educating students. Most of the students at East Coast are there for a multitude of reasons, all similarly involved with the problems which now exist in terms of the education offered by our higher institutions. East Coast students were fed up with the same old methods of learning by listening to lectures and writing endless term papers. East Coast students were fed up with: (1) taking examinations to qualify (2) to take other examinations to qualify for certain courses (3) to qualify for writing a dissertation (4) to qualify to take a comprehensive oral examination (5) to finally obtain an advanced degree! East Coast students were fed up with following minutely the "advice" of advisors, as much as they were fed up with taking some 30 to 40 different graduate courses out of which only approximately 10 to 20 percent would have any value in the professional role being prepared for. This university is a Graduate and Postgraduate School which allows students to complete independent work in a program designed for them as individuals. The student is expected to complete individual study and research programs through a combination of summer resident research, individual study, seminars, lectures, discussions, conferences and off-campus periods of independent study done either at home or at another college or university. In connection with this, East Coast operates on a 12-month basis, so that students may matriculate and begin work off-campus at any time before or after fulfilling resident requirements during a summer session. East Coast University suggests that students pursue courses at other colleges for which credit will be given toward a graduate degree and, in fact, insists only that a minimum of 16 resident credits be completed at the university. The student arranges his own individual program with an advisor, and the uniqueness of the program allows the student to pursue in-depth research in the area of his own choosing in his field of concentration. While there is complete absence of required or listed courses which a candidate is expected to complete, each student is expected to thoroughly investigate all available research material in his field. The required resident study is largely self-directed, and may be fulfilled during summer sessions. The only other requirement for the advanced degree in education is that at least seven years' experience have been gained in the field.

The university has been operating successfully and degree programs have been completed by many students who, previously, were limited in their pursuit of an advanced degree by personality differences with an advisor which resulted in non-acceptance of their dissertation. There are also many administrators who have been able to complete degree requirements at East Coast which they would not have been able to do elsewhere because of the severe limitations on the amount of time they could spend in residence. Ironically, a number of professors from other colleges and universities have chosen to work toward their advanced degrees at East Coast. Experiences have proven that seminars at this university are more valuable in content than those offered at the more traditionally oriented universities and colleges across the country. At present, the University of Massachusetts is attempting to implement a similar program, and the colleges and universities of the future will probably employ these concepts to the fullest extent possible.

The Imaginary Cafeteria

In order to truly individualize and humanize education, students must be able to select the materials (interest levels) which suit them best. It would be appropriate, for purposes of clarification, to equate nongraded, individualized education with an imaginary cafeteria. Students enter a cafeteria because they are hungry for food and, in an ideal situation, students go to school because they are hungry for knowledge. In a cafeteria, various foods are arranged attractively so that the hungry student may select those items which are most appealing to him. He exercises great care in making his selection of the proper nutrients containing the necessary carbohydrates, proteins, minerals, calcium, and vitamins to keep his body in peak condition. In no less manner should the school be able to place a variety of materials containing the nutrients of education before the student so that he may make a choice of those which are most appealing to him. Even as utensils with which to eat are selected by the student in the cafeteria, so should he be able to select those learning utensils which will enable him best to ensnare the "food of knowledge." As a more pertinent example, let us suppose the topic being studied was "Man and His Universe." The materials from which the student is to make his selection should include a number of books, pamphlets and articles about man and his universe, with different titles by different authors with different styles of writing. When this array is placed before the student, he is better able to choose that which he can best grasp and absorb. How much wiser is this method than placing before the student one motley bowl of food which may be totally unpalatable to him and which, consequently, he either rejects outright or will be unable to digest. The after-effects of a meal in our imaginary cafeteria are comparable to those of partaking of knowledge in a school where individualized instruction is adhered to — the student leaves the cafeteria well-sated and, having had a pleasant experience, will return again. So would this author have students leave school after having had pleasant experiences in learning, well-sated for a time, but eager to return again, rather than lapsing into those habits of tardiness and absence with which educators are all too familiar. When the imaginary cafeteria schematic becomes commonplace in public schools, as opposed to the rarity it now is, nongraded schools will really be implementing programs geared to meeting the interests and needs of each student within their halls.

SUMMARY

The nongraded curriculum must be directed toward and oriented to the child as a unique individual, and must take into account his experiences in his society and in his community. There are three basic formats for nongraded curriculum in existence in public schools which have adopted the nongraded concept of education: the Skill Concept Sequence Plan; the Individual Study Unit Plan; and the Multiple Phase Plan. Each plan attempts to individualize the instructional program in a different way, and each one has certain advantages balanced against certain disadvantages. However, any one of the three plans is to be considered an improvement over the traditional curriculum which does not recognize individual differences among students. A most important aspect of the nongraded curriculum is the opportunity of choice which is presented to the student so that he may decide what he is to learn and from which materials he will be learning.

6. ORGANIZING

THE CLASSROOM

FOR NONGRADED

EDUCATION

Students must supplement large-group instruction and small-group discussion with individual work. They need time to broaden their perceptual base, to continue the development of concepts, skills, and attitudes and to communicate through reading, writing, listening and recording. They need time for evaluation.

Dorothy Westby Gibson

Today, when there is an emphasis on individualization of instruction, flexible scheduling, modular scheduling and team teaching, hundreds of school districts throughout the country are spending billions of dollars in the construction of traditional egg-crate type school buildings which have actually become obsolete before the first brick is laid. Many of these conventional buildings are neither imaginative in design nor created to afford maximum flexibility. Reluctant school administrators continue to waste taxpayers' money by taking a staid attitude of maintaining the status quo, rather than accommodating the needs for large group instruction, medium group instruction, small group instruction and independent study in a basic structure suitable to contemporary education. This chapter is written to suggest certain methods by which the design of physical plants may be somewhat standardized to afford maximum opportunities for flexibility.

The first consideration which must be made is that the nongraded classroom is and must be different from the traditional classroom. The traditional classroom is built to accommodate 30 youngsters in a grouped arrangement which may or may not be divided. The seats are usually in restrictive orderly fashion which dictates one seat for the teacher, and one particular seat for each student. A seating plan is prepared by the teacher and serves as identification of a student because he happens to be seated in a particular place. In contrast, the nongraded classroom student is not assigned to any particular seat or desk. Each seat and desk is there for the use of any student who may choose to use it. Restriction to one seat is shunned, and each student must be identified by his individual characteristics. The author recommends either one of two ways to organize classrooms for nongraded education – self-contained classroom, or cluster classroom patterns.

Self-Contained Nongraded Classroom

The following is an explanation of the various sections of a self-contained nongraded classroom as illustrated in Figure 6-1 on page 111 and is intended only as a guide; administrators may wish to deviate from it or adopt an entirely new pattern, dependent upon the needs of their particular school population.

(a) In this section, there are four individual study carrels situated for independent study. Note that the backs of the chairs are placed so they face the walls to afford students as much privacy as possible. Film projectors may be utilized in the area to view film-strips individually, since the carrels can easily accommodate a film-strip projector, as well as a tape recorder or a phonograph. When the tape recorder or phonograph is being used, it would be wise to provide an individual headset attachment which eliminates the possibility of distracting noise interference. These carrels may also be utilized by students for work on programmed instruction units, for reading, and for the completion of individual study units. Obviously, the carrels would be appropriate for any efforts which require independent or individual study.

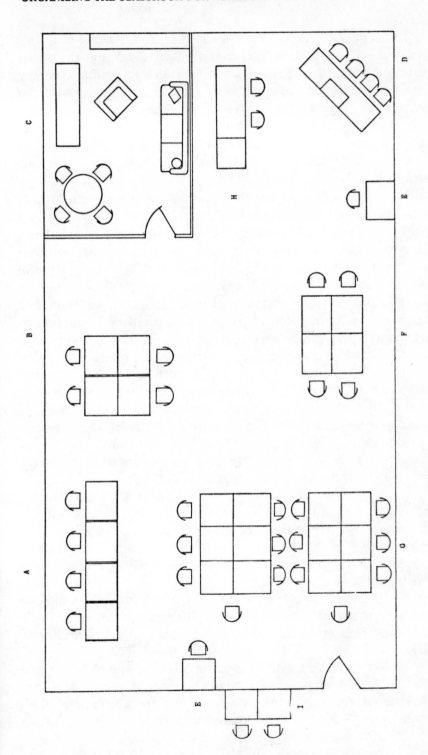

Figure 6-1. *Self-contained nongraded classroom.*

(b) Three or four common interest tables are arranged in this section so that students with common interests and similar abilities can be sub-grouped in a small working area. Audio-visual aids may easily be situated on these tables to provide all students with the opportunity for viewing as required. These tables can also accommodate a tape recorder which can be fitted with multi-connective trunks to individual headsets for each child which permit several to listen to a particular tape simultaneously without distraction.

(c) In this section, a comfortable area for relaxation is located in the corner and includes a couch, arm chairs and pillows situated much as they would be in a living room. A small coffee table in front of the sofa may hold school or class reading materials. Students are permitted to visit this area whenever they have free time and/or the desire to read for pleasure or class work.

(d) This is the instructional television section. With the existence of a central control room for transmitting instruction to students, this area can be used quite effectively. The central control can facilitate the transmission of pre-arranged instructional material to students at prearranged times. Unfortunately, most school districts do not use educational television as much as they should or in the many ways they could. This lapse is expensive, for since it is necessary to invest a rather large sum to install the television system, it ought to be used to the fullest possible extent. The use of television can be quite effective as a supplementary tool to aid teachers in individualization of instruction.

(e) In this section, isolated areas such as these are located throughout the classroom and are excellent for students working independently or under the direction of the teacher. Students should be permitted to make their own choice with regard to using this area and, quite often, students who are introverts will find these areas more attractive than any other.

(f) In this section, seminars or small group instruction may be conducted. Areas such as these are ideal for reading instruction by a teacher, or for a group of students who wish to practice reading to one another.

(g) Here a teacher gathers together students who have common interests. A student remains in charge of one group as the teacher moves about the classroom giving guidance to other groups. This section is ideal for work on study units, small or medium group instruction, or completion of individual study units.

(h) A Movie Mover located in this section can be used primarily for the presentation of 16 millimeter films, to supplement instruction in various subject areas.

(i) Outside of the classroom, this section can be utilized in a team learning situation — "Two or three chairs and a desk may be placed together so that students having a project in common may work with each other." Working in this area demands on the part of the students a certain trustworthiness and responsibility which the teacher should make every effort to foster and encourage.

The organizational pattern of the self-contained classroom is such that it is possible for children to function individually at various levels and skills in any subject. In a classroom of 28 to 30 youngsters, each may be supplied with an individual study unit which has been compiled by reviewing placement and pre-tests. These tests determine the level at which a student is functioning and his deficiencies. It is then possible to pick out sections or segments of units in a particular subject area which he needs and thereby design an individual study unit for this particular student. Teachers and students are responsible for the grouping arrangement which can and should be extremely flexible so that each child, upon completion of his individual study unit, may or may not remain with the particular group to which he was originally assigned. The unit on which the student is working, the number of students in a particular group, the student's choice, and the teacher's consideration of educational feasibility all combine to determine a student's location.

The following is an example of a reading program in the same self-contained nongraded classroom:

The area designated A is one which is designed for the utilization of visual perception skills. A language master and recording cards which have been pre-recorded by the teacher are available for student use, and initially, students are told to bring in pictures of objects beginning with a particular letter of the alphabet, which they identify and then paste on the recorder cards. The teacher then records the word on the recorder card and writes it under the picture, after which the properly recorded card may be used by each student to play back, see and hear the work, following which he may then record the word himself several times. The student may continue working with a word, erasing the incorrect pronunciations until he achieves the pronunciation recorded by the teacher.

The area designated B is being used for measuring phonics analysis skills. The tape recorder on the table has a central control which can receive multi-jacks from headsets supplied to students. In this manner, students are able to play a tape and listen to the teacher's recitation of certain short or long words which the students identify in their individual study units by drawing a line under the word they think they have heard.

Area C is being used by students who are reading for pleasure. One is relaxing on the comfortable sofa while others are using the arm chairs, and several are reclining on the rug. These students, who may be further advanced than their classmates, are permitted to select reading material of their own choice such as poetry or novels and retire to this area to read independently.

Area D, equipped with educational television, is being used by students viewing a film on the use of the dictionary on television while using individual headsets which permit them to hear without disturbing students engaged in other activities. Here again, individual study units have been coupled with the visual demonstration of dictionary use, for example, and the students are enabled to work toward the completion of the individual study sheets which each one has concerning the proper use of the dictionary.

In area E both students are working independently on their individual study units. Each student is building structural analysis skills through observance of the effect or meaning of a verb when an appendage such as "ing" is added. The students are deciding on a root word and coupling it with an appropriate ending to achieve clarity.

In area F, a teacher aide is working with students practicing alphabetizing. After the teacher spends about ten or fifteen minutes with the group, the teacher aide then serves as a sounding board for the verbal recitation of letters of the alphabet by students.

In area G, six students are practicing work-study skills with the teacher who proceeds orally from easy directions to more difficult directions, after which she aids these students in locating information, using selective and evaluative skills, and organizing information for recall.

Area H is being utilized by a student for viewing an oral communication via a 16 millimeter film on the Movie Mover. Individual study units provide a task relating to the film which the student is to complete immediately after viewing the film.

In area I, two students are assigned to work in a team learning situation where each will provide help to the other. Jointly, they will plan an original story by drawing pictures and supplying the dialogue, both of which are then recorded to be played back to the teacher and to the rest of the class. Every student will have an opportunity to participate in a team learning situation similar to this so that all may learn the value of living, playing and working together cooperatively.

Clusters of Nongraded Classrooms

For administrators who desire the maximum use of the educational physical plant, the author recommends a nongraded procedure which utilizes clusters of classrooms. The creative administrator, of course, may want to alter or modify the following plan according to his needs and the needs of his student and teacher population. Figure 6-2 on page 116 indicates the manner in which a cluster of traditional classrooms may be set up to provide the necessary flexibility in the physical plant to accomplish the implementation of the nongraded concept. In order to remodel the traditional classroom the administrator will need to solicit the board of education for its approval of certain modifications in the physical plant. A first step in this direction would be the organization of a team of teachers who would meet with a qualified architect, superintendent of buildings or other knowledgeable person, to review existing physical plant arrangements and to arrive at a decision on the removal of certain walls and other modifications which will ensure flexibility. Once such a plan has been designed, presented to and approved by the board of education, renovation should be started during the summer months so that there is ample time to complete construction prior to the inception of the school year in September. The organizational pattern described below may be used for clusters of traditional classrooms which have or have not been modified or renovated to permit such use.

The classroom in Area A is designed to permit independent study. Approximately 25 to 30 "hot-dry" (wired and unwired) study carrels have been located in this classroom. Specially designated areas, easily accessible, should be provided with educational equipment such as the Language Master, tape recorders, sound filmstrips, phonographs, and various other aids to learning.

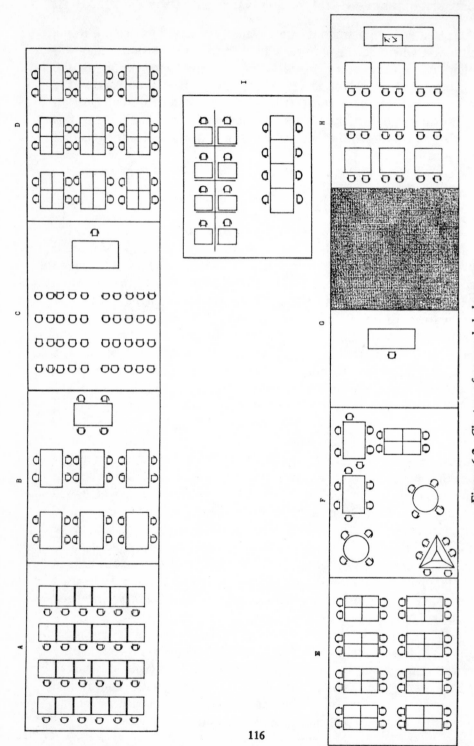

Figure 6-2. *Clusters of nongraded classrooms.*

Area B is designed to accommodate medium-sized group instruction for 25 to 40 students. A 16 millimeter projector, an overhead projector, an opaque projector and a Du Kane projector should be stored permanently in this area for possible use. Whenever there is no actual necessity for using the auditorium, this room can be used.

In Area C, medium group instruction for 40 students or more may be provided and, again, this room may be used in lieu of the auditorium or cafeteria. In this room, a teacher would usually lecture or discuss content of work which is mutually beneficial to a large number of students.

Area D has room for sundry small group activities such as team learning, small group instruction, common interest projects, various instructional and special needs. Although there would usually be no equipment in this classroom this does not, however, limit the teacher who wishes to bring in equipment. In this classroom, one classroom aide would normally assist the teacher.

Areas E and H are also designed for small group activities; also, they are well equipped with conglomerate tools of educational technology such as television, computer, Movie Mover, Du Kane projector and calculators, to mention a few. It seems plausible at this point to discuss the role which educational technology will play in modernizing education. At present, many parents and educators are unaware of the major role which educational technology will assume as more and more administrators begin to emphasize the individualization of instruction. As a supplement to the teacher bent on individualizing instruction, the tools of educational technology are of major importance. However, the public must be educated to look upon these tools as something more than just another gimmick, and widespread acceptance must be gained for the basic idea that to-day's complex educative processes cannot be accomplished efficiently by a teacher working alone without the supplementary aid these tools provide.

Area F is a multi-purpose area equipped with a variety of furniture ranging from trapezoidal to round to rectangular tables with an adequate number of chairs. This room may be used for a host of educational activities such as producing material for plays to be presented by students, educational games, learning activities, panel discussions, and debating team sessions.

The room designated Area G can be used for small group instruction and reading sessions. The shared area should be equipped with a minimum of furniture, perhaps only a teacher's desk or table. Part of this room should have wall-to-wall carpeting on which students may relax and listen to the teacher or to other students who may be making a presentation. The uncarpeted area may be used by the teacher for a number of instructional devices to better work-study skills. For instance, a teacher might recite directions, ranging from simple to complex, for students to follow. Depending upon the teacher's ingenuity, a number of other educational activities can be accomplished here.

Area I is a planning area for teachers. Here, such teacher may have his own personal planning area, equipped with a desk, chair, and filing cabinets, separated by a partition to allow privacy. A large table should also be available in this area for planning conferences in which a group of teachers may be engaged.

The foregoing guides for various uses and accommodations of the physical plant have been designed to aid the administrator and teachers in fostering a program for individualizing and personalizing instruction. It should be remembered, however, that regardless of whether the physical plant is traditional or contemporary in design, the key to adequacy is flexibility. The instructional program must be able to meet the needs of the instructional staff in an accommodative environment in order to satisfy the individual needs of all the children.

Team Teaching

This book has dealt specifically with the nongraded concept and all its aspects. It is appropriate at this point to add another dimension to the concept which will enhance the educational program by the proper utilization of teaching staff, particularly if the clusters of nongraded classrooms are the chosen organizational pattern of the educational program. Most students have peaks and valleys to which their individual talents and abilities either rise or fall. For example, one student may be excellent in reading but poor in mathematics, while another student may be only fair in social studies but outstanding in science. Teaching a student as if his talents and abilities were the same in each discipline is educationally unsound. Every student should be assessed separately in each subject area, so that appropriate determinations may be made for initiating the teaching program. Just as students have their valleys and peaks in the country of learning, so, too, does the teacher have her valleys and peaks in her country of teaching. Where no allowance is made for either the heights or depths in student learning and teacher teaching, only intellectual waste can result. Even as the public school system has allowed school to become irrelevant for many of today's youngsters, so have the public schools done nothing to compensate for the peaks and valleys which each teacher possesses in her professional preparation. For instance, a teacher who was assigned to a self-contained classroom and happened to be poor in arithmetic was simply told, arbitrarily, to perform in the manner she was best capable of in her weak area. Quite obviously, the students assigned to this teacher suffered for one full year because of this teacher's deficiency. We all know how this affects the later school career. It could have been avoided.

Today, more and more administrators are attempting to compensate for the teacher valleys and peaks by coordinating the efforts of a number of teachers as a team. Team teaching is the process of arranging the instructional time of teachers and learners by appropriately grouping them in terms of variety of peak talents in different disciplines and merging them as it were, to make a highly knowledgeable multi-teacher. Team teaching is a thoroughly humanistic and realistic approach to teacher capabilities, for it admits of the fact that it is an extremely rare teacher who is an expert in every subject area. Unfortunately, some schools have misinterpreted team teaching so that it resembles only departmentalization, if it is observed in a high school where there is a mathematics teacher, a science teacher, etc. In addition, other administrators have incorrectly translated team teaching into "turn teaching," where teachers take turns teaching in various subject areas to groups of students. Most specifically, team teaching is a process in which each teacher assumes the responsibility of educating two or more students through the use of a cooperative teaching method to achieve mutually agreed-upon objectives, and arrives at a joint evaluation of the degree to which the objectives have been accomplished. Team teaching consists of cooperative planning, teaching, and evaluation.

At this point, it might be useful to the reader to describe the basic composition of students in a team teaching situation:

1. Independent Study – consisting of 1 student working independently.

2. Small Group Instruction – consisting of approximately 15 students working together.

3. Medium Group Instruction – consisting of 25 to 40 students.

4. Large Group Instruction – consisting of approximately 100 or more students.

There follows an illustration of how team teaching might work in a particular school district.

The administrator has arranged for the teachers to be in the school building approximately one hour prior to student arrival. This time is set aside for the planning of team teaching scope and depth for the day. Usually, there will be approximately three to five teachers per team, dependent upon the general characteristics or composition of the school. Each of these teams would be assigned a block of students. In a school district somewhat restricted in the use of its funds, there might be 120 students assigned to four teachers. In more affluent school districts, we would have these four teachers assisted by a couple of teacher aides. Functionally, this setup would operate as follows:

Organizational Patterns

Imagine that 180 students form the circumference of a pie-like circle. At the center of the pie would be six teachers and four teacher aides. For purposes of this hypothesis, we will think in terms of the mathematics discipline. One of the teachers who is more proficient in verbalization or lecturing to large groups would be elected to teach a large segment of the pie composed of approximately 110 students. Not only would his duties consist of making verbal presentations to these students, but this teacher might also make effective use of 16 millimeter film, opaque projectors, and film slides. The balance of the fictive pie would then be sliced into student segments as follows:

Approximately 15 students needing remedial work would constitute a wedge with whom a teacher and a teacher aide would pursue remedial work. Another wedge would consist of approximately 14 students, working with special instruction in a particular phase of the lesson which has been introduced to the larger group. Approximately 6 students who are far advanced enough to engage in individualized instruction or independent study without teacher supervision would constitute another wedge of the hypothetical pie. These students would probably be located in the library following research or using carrels to work on their special projects. The final wedge would consist of approximately 35 students in a medium group situation who are not extremely advanced, but are somewhat further advanced than those students receiving large group instruction. A teacher and a teacher aide would work closely with these students providing the relevant instruction.

Physical accommodations for students in the team teaching situation might be handled through the assignment, on the first day of school, of students to various large rooms in the school. These might consist of the auditorium, the gymnasium, or the cafeteria. Each of these would be considered as the circle or block of students for each team. At this time, an inventory test should be administered to the entire block of students for particular discipline. One of the teachers might preside during this phase, while the others might be circulating with teacher aides to assist students and see that they are following directions. Other teachers might be arranging the rooms which are to receive students, while still others might be making arrangements for the acquisition of necessary tools of educational technology, equipment, etc., to be used as teacher aids. At present, the nongraded cluster classroom would seem to be the most appropriate design pattern for effective team teaching. There is a good chance that the student will not complete the inventory examination within the same day and it may be necessary to carry it over to the following day. However, if possible, testing should be completed on the same day, so that the next morning teachers may meet to decide how students will be grouped for independent study, or for small, medium or large group instruction.

The teachers will find that, as they work with students, certain corrections in their placement can and should be made. At times, criteria for grouping must be changed. The caution here is that large group instruction should be performed by a master teacher who has the ability to speak to large groups with clarity and ease. Again, no group or teacher assignment should be permanent. A particular assignment should continue only so long as team members judge the arrangement to be the most efficient and productive. Constant surveillance should be maintained by the administrator to see that maximum learning is taking place. There are various methods of team teaching, and entire volumes have been devoted to this topic. The author's comments were made only to be certain that recognition of the value of team teaching was impressed upon professionals.

Multi-Age Grouping

Many school districts that have organized the nongraded concept around the self-contained classroom, have found that multi-age grouping has been an effective device for improving the educational program in nongraded schools for the following reasons:

1. It induces the teacher to individualize the instructional program to suit a class composed of heterogeneously grouped students.

2. Various discipline problems within the group tend to diminish.

3. There is a high degree of cooperation among all children in the class, regardless of age or ability. This is particularly true in terms of those students who may be older by approximately two years than others in the class, because what has developed in these cases is the "big brother"/"big sister" attitude.

4. There also tends to be a greater degree of independence and individual initiative on the part of the teacher and students in the class.

5. In each classroom, group work and committees can be organized with less delay and with more efficiency because of the leadership which evolves on the part of the older students.

6. A closer to normal situation is provided where students are exposed to other students who differ in age within a two or three year age range. This is the kind of situation to which children are accustomed at home with brothers and sisters, or at play in the community with peers, and one which renders the school setting more natural.

When multi-aged students are chosen at random, heterogeneously grouped, and assigned to a particular teacher, some of the artificiality is removed from the school setting. Usually, the age span ranges from a two to three year difference. In Appleton, Wisconsin, the Appleton Public Schools have used multi-age grouping extensively throughout all their schools and the success of their program has been noted in many journal articles. A closer examination of the organizational patterns of these situations reveals that a nongraded environment may exist either in a self-contained or a cluster classroom. Team teaching allows for the proper utilization of teachers. Multi-age grouping, which organizes students in a situation more compatible with their daily existence, has been proven to be the more effective approach to nongraded teaching. Even if there seems to be inadequate available space to implement a nongraded program in what was formerly a traditionally oriented school, consideration of making the change should not be discarded until efforts to utilize "unused" portions of the school building, such as the halls, basement, and alcoves have been explored. In many of the nongraded schools which the author visited, the school administrators had made use of these normally unused portions of the school plant. In one school, the halls were used to accommodate carrels where students worked on independent projects; in another the alcoves were used for team learning by students who congregated together to learn from each other. In still another school, the administrator had given directions to the custodial staff which resulted in transforming the basement into an attractive, multi-purpose room. In addition, the cafeteria and the auditorium, which are usually never fully utilized during the school day, are sources of extra space. Aside from the above sources of space, additional space may be acquired by demolishing several walls between classrooms. For the administrator seeking to provide a flexible physical plant to foster the nongraded concept, a quick look around the average school building is enough to reveal countless "wasted" spaces which can be put to use. When all of the above considerations have been taken into account and there still seems to be insufficient space to accommodate the nongraded program, it may be necessary to delay implementation of the nongraded program in order to plan for renovation or expansion of physical facilities. If this is necessary, the wise administrator would do well to plan with an eye toward future needs. Overcrowded classrooms should not constitute a final and irrevocable excuse for not exploring the nongraded concept for, after all, where there is a will there is a way, just as necessity is the mother of invention. Of course, if a new building is contemplated, every opportunity should be made to provide administrators and teachers with an opportunity to visit contemporary schools to bring back insights and suggestions. Strongly recommended also, is attendance at the American Association of School Administrators' regular annual conference in Atlantic City, usually held in February, where a wealth of school architects' displays may be observed. The Association also makes available film clips showing school building design which may be obtained by addressing a request to them at 1201 Sixteenth Street, N.W., Washington, D.C. They are also helpful in providing information about where certain school architectural firms are located. The author has observed that, unfortunately, the East Coast has not been as progressive in school plant design as has the West Coast and it may be necessary to travel West to observe school buildings which are most progressive, both in design and structure.

SUMMARY

It is absolutely necessary that American educators begin to update the physical plant as part of providing a flexible program of education to meet the needs of individual students. While this is never a simple or inexpensive procedure, it is a necessary procedure if total effectiveness is to be achieved. There are, at present, two basic methods by which the physical plant may meet the needs of the nongraded concept, i.e., by providing either a self-contained classroom, or a cluster of classrooms. The self-contained classroom is basically designed for use in elementary schools, while the cluster of classrooms may prove useful in either elementary or secondary schools. Regardless of the method used, flexibility must be always kept in mind as being of the utmost importance when effectively organizing the physical plant to suit the needs of students and teachers working in a nongraded atmosphere.

The organizational pattern of the nongraded classroom is enhanced if team teaching and multi-age grouping have been effectively introduced in the program. Where the self-contained classroom is a feature of the design pattern of the particular school, multi-age grouping is recommended in order for teachers to fully accommodate the individuality of students. It also serves as an inducement to teachers to individualize the instructional program. Where a cluster nongraded classroom has been included in the organizational pattern, team teaching is recommended not only for the purpose of properly utilizing the teaching staff, but also to accrue the benefits that result from segregation of a number of students in order to meet their varied, individual needs more fully.

7. INDIVIDUALIZING THE INSTRUCTIONAL PROGRAM

. . .liberate a student from the lockstep . . . let him move forward at his own best pace and go on as far as he can, release teachers from much of the routine of exposition and drill and let them concentrate on smoothing and enriching the progress of individual students.

Wilbur Schramm

In traditional education, too much emphasis has been placed upon attempting to teach the mass of students. Contemporarily, it is of primary importance that the emphasis be refocused on teaching the individual student. As times change, so must the areas of educational emphasis. It will not be easy for all teachers to change their attitudes about teaching, because traditional methods of education have been so embedded in the minds of many educators that for them there seems to be no alternate method. Even for those who can envision the possibilities of individualized teaching methods, the old habits make it difficult to adjust to the demands of education in a contemporary society which must adapt itself to meet the individual needs of its members. It is the author's intent in this chapter to provide the reader with an overview of some of the tools and techniques with which to individualize instruction. It is suggested, however, that an educator contemplating the use of any of the items referred to do so at first only in limited quantities on a trial basis as it were, to determine the potential effectiveness of the particular educational tool in his school milieu before making large-scale purchases.

Flexibility in the Nongraded Classroom

Just as new methods of instruction must be initiated, new materials, equipment, and furniture must be utilized in order to fully meet student needs. The following items have proven successful as aids to teachers in nongraded programs:

Recommended Furniture:

1. Student desks and chairs (standard equipment);
2. Rectangular tables (to be used for small group instruction and other activities);
3. Half-round tables (to provide flexibility in use of furniture; i.e., they can be joined together whenever a larger, round, discussion table will best serve educational purposes).

Highly Desirable:

1. Carrels for undistracted, independent study;
2. Trapezoidal tables (to extend flexibility);
3. Mobile book carts;
4. Room dividers (to section off portions of the class for various grouped activities);
5. Couch and lounge chairs (for relaxing while reading).

Recommended Equipment:

1. *Overhead projector and screen.* The overhead projector is one of the most recent major advances to augment a teacher's classroom effectiveness in imparting her knowledge to students in a manner which will assure the utmost in retention by them. The projector also allows a teacher to instruct one group of students without disturbing other students set off in a far corner area.

2. *Tape recorder.* The tape recorder allows each student to learn at his own pace, permitting the class to listen to the daily lesson on tape, while accelerated students move ahead to advanced lessons, and remedial students can work on still another assignment. The teacher then has ample freedom to supervise each group's progress. The tape recorder can be effectively used in many subject areas, such as foreign languages, social science, etc.

3. *Filmstrip projector.* This piece of equipment, involving the use of filmstrips, record player and earphones, is ideal for individual or small group instruction of a maximum of four students. The equipment can be utilized without disturbing the rest of the class and can be operated by push-button remote control, or manually.

4. *The phonograph.* The record player can be used as a single educational machine for listening instructional purposes, as well as for visual instructional purposes, in conjunction with the filmstrip projector.

Highly Desirable:

1. *The Language Master.* The Language Master is basically a tape recorder. However, instead of being equipped with nylon tapes, it uses cards to record messages. There are sets of pre-recorded cards and also blank cards which afford the instructor a variety of prepared or original materials. Obvious flexibility for instructor and students can be achieved by incorporating original supplemental materials on the blank cards. The Language Master may be used at all grade levels, by the instructor in group instruction, or individually by the student for progression at his own rate.

2. *The Craig Reader.* The Craig Reader, patterned after a miniature television set, designed for individual use with little or no supervision, utilizes slides to project programmed materials and permits the student to select his own reading speed while viewing the reading lesson line by line, which prevents rereading or regressing.

   3. *Controlled Reader.* The Controlled Reader utilizes a moving slot traveling across a screen from left to right, and improves visual mobility and concentration, interpretive skills and comprehension.

   4. *Tachistocopic Projector.* Visual discrimination skills and stabilization of a sight vocabulary are enhanced by the Tachistocopic Projector, which also helps the older student to increase his visual perception and retention.

   5. *The Aud-X.* The Aud-X allows a student to assimilate new words on a screen while listening to an interesting story, absorbing them in his individual way through the auto-instructional capability of the Aud-X which provides pronunciation, graphic and sound qualities of new words in a unique sight-sound synchronization.

   6. *Autotutor.* The Autotutor with its Tutorfilm study units is a sophisticated teaching machine providing programmed instruction in a series of "frames," which are automatically presented to the student on the basis of his correct or incorrect response to the preceding question. New material is presented to the student only when he has demonstrated proper understanding of earlier material by making the correct response. The Autotutor provides a student with either remedial or advanced work according to his need, and can serve to dramatically increase motivation.

   7. *Closed Circuit Television with Headsets.* The advantages to be gained through use of educational television are obvious, and the author believes it unnecessary to burden the reader with them here since everyone has observed the intensity, alacrity and retention which television inspires in the modern American student.

Instructional Materials:

   1. *Placement Test.* Before any individualization of instruction can take place in the nongraded classroom, the teacher must determine the proper placement level for each child. In order to accomplish this, a placement or inventory test must be administered to each child in each subject area. While self-constructed individual tests

may be prepared and administered by staff members, since devising the tests is usually a lengthy, time-consuming process, the author recommends the use of commercially prepared tests. The following tests are deserving of consideration in making a choice as to the most effective measuring instrument:

The Botel Reading Inventory provides proper placement of pupils in books they can read with profit so that they may better progress in reading skills. The Reading Placement and Phonics Mastery tests help the teacher to determine the proper Instructional Level at which the pupil may progress with teacher guidance; the Free Reading Level at which the pupil can read without teacher guidance; and the Frustration Level at which a pupil cannot read with profit, even with teacher aid.

2. *Textbooks.* While textbooks are not the primary teaching tool in the nongraded classroom, they are one of the many instructional elements which play a major part in the success or failure of any nongraded program. However, textbooks for nongraded education must of necessity assume a different role and even a different form than they would in traditional education.

Administrators must use all of their ingenuity to induce teachers to maintain a program of individualized instruction even though textbooks are being utilized. One effective method used by a nongraded school principal was a procedure whereby no more than four books of the same publisher were allowed to be used on a particular level. For example, only four textbooks published by Eureka Publishing Company would be permitted for use at the lower level, in combination with only four textbooks of as many other publishers as were necessary to provide ample texts for class population. This procedure would apply to all levels and concomitantly to all subject areas in order that teachers might provide a variety of textual resources for students.

3. *Pocket-Books.* An alternate technique which has been used successfully involved the introduction of paperback pocket-books to be used in the classroom. Much variety may be provided inexpensively in this manner and the small paperbacks hold a certain attraction for most students. In one school utilizing individualized instruction techniques, students are required to read ten such paperbacks and submit book reports on each as part of their term work in English. Another point in favor of the use of paperbacks which is not to be minimized is the immense flexibility in content which is provided at a very limited expense.

4. *Educational Kits.* A number of companies have been preparing educational kits in various subject series to supplement classroom instructional techniques. These consist of a series of lessons geared to progressive levels in a particular subject area which can be used to individualize the instructional program. For facility in use and identification the series are usually color coded to represent various levels of ability at a glance. Each selection at a particular level comes equipped with a guide for its use, together with appropriate tests included in a student record book. Among the companies manufacturing these kits are Science Research Associates, Inc., and New Dimensions in Education, of Jericho, New York, the latter of which has recently added the "new dimensions" of filmstrips, 16 millimeter films, and records to their educational kits. This trend will probably soon be reflected in the offerings of other similar films.

5. *Programmed Materials.* These aids eliminate a great deal of routine from teacher performance, by substituting programmed instruction for teacher instruction. The programmed instruction equipment, which was first developed and used successfully by behavioral psychologists in laboratory experimentation, is designed to lead the student through a series of responses to multiple choice questions, after he has read related material. The questions are posed

sequentially, in a series of step-by-step added information, in a manner which permits the student to see the correct answer after he has made his choice. The method. because of its step-by-step procedures, permits a student to make correct responses most of the time, eliminating the frustration of incorrect answers and providing immediate gratification for correct answers. In other words, the programmed instructional materials are designed to lead students through a specific behavior pattern which will help them to provide correct responses to queries about information which they have absorbed. The benefits of programmed techniques and materials in education were stated most succinctly by Ernest R. Hilgard:

> Programmed learning recognizes individual differences by beginning where the learner is and by permitting him to proceed at his own pace. It is possible that programmed learning may succeed in reducing individual differences because of these features.
>
> Programmed learning requires that the learner be active. Learning by doing is an old educational adage, and it is still a good one. The teaching machine (or program in book form) fights the tendency for the student to be passive and inattentive by requiring his participation if the lesson is to move.
>
> Programmed learning provides immediate knowledge of results. Whether because it provides reinforcement, reward, or cognitive feedback (to use some of the words that experts use in talking about these matters), there is abundant testimony that an instantaneous report of results is important in learning.
>
> Programmed learning emphasizes the organized nature of knowledge because it requires continuity between the easier (earlier) concepts and the harder (later) ones.
>
> Programmed learning provides spaced review in order to guarantee the high order of success that has become a standard requirement of

good programs. Review with applications, if properly arranged, permits a high order of learning on the first run through the program.

Programmed learning reduces anxiety because the learner is not threatened by the task; he is learning what is required and gains the satisfaction that this knowledge brings.[1]

Some of the more effectively developed programmed materials are:

1. Scholastic Self Training Arithmetic

2. Encyclopedia Britannica Temac Programmed Texts

3. Censo Programmed Learner

4. Science Research Associates Programmed Instruction in Science

5. MacAlaster Honor Programmed Subject Rolls

6. Webster Programmed Reading Books

7. McGraw-Hill Programmed Reading Books

8. Behavioral Research Laboratory Programmed Materials

9. Harcourt, Brace and World's English 2600

Other educational materials which aid the instructional program and help to individualize instruction are:

1. Webster Classroom Reading Clinic

2. Science Research Associates Reading Laboratory

3. SRA Kaleidoscope of Skills (varied subject areas)

4. SRA Pilot Library

5. SRA Reading for Understanding

6. Merrill Building Reading Power Kit

7. E.D.L. Study Skills Library

---

[1] Ernest R. Hilgard, "Teaching Machines and Creativity," *Stanford Today*, Vol. 1, Autumn, 1963.

8. Merrill Skill Tapes/Skill Text

9. Encyclopedia Britannica – The Literature Game

10. SRA Computational Skills Development Kit

11. SRA Cross Number Puzzle Boxes

12. SRA Equations

13. SRA Inquiry Box

14. SRA Learning in Science Kit

15. 100 Invitations to Investigate

16. Holt, Rinehart, Co., Physical Science Kit

17. Baker Science Packet

18. SRA Basic Skills Series Kit

19. SRA Graph and Picture Study Skills Kit

20. SRA Map and Globe Skills Kit

21. SRA Spelling Word Power Laboratory

22. SRA Penskill

6. *Simulating Learning Games.* An extremely efficient technique to be incorporated into methods of individualized instruction is the simulation of certain real elements of some object or process which is to be learned. This is accomplished by extracting the essential features of the process and incorporating them into a simulated model which is perhaps more relevant and less complex, but is representative of the function of the original. Once the basic principle on which the simulated model functions is absorbed, it can then be transferred and applied to the actual functions of the original. The simulation technique can be extremely successful in science education, particularly if it is combined with tools of computerized education. It also provides a great deal of flexibility to an instructor who seeks to expose students to certain learning experiences which, under realistic conditions, would include too many operational complexities to be readily assimilated by novices. Simulated learning experiences are highly recommended as instructional aides for students who

are culturally different, because of the opportunity to translate objects and processes which are to be learned into the terms of a relevant meaningful atmosphere or condition for the student. While it is advisable, wherever feasible, for the instructor to create "simulations" which are relevant to his students, some very fine learning games have been placed on the market, among them the following:

Social Movement	Fairleigh Dickinson College, Rutherford, N. J.
Manchester Empire	Educational Development Corporation, Brattle Square, Cambridge, Massachusetts
Investment Banking Real Estate And others	All of these are bookshelf games, manufactured by 3 M Manufacturing Company and readily available at department stores.

Individualization of instruction can become an integral part of the educational program only when the teacher desires it and works actively to make it permeate all areas of her instructional day. Every tool in the classroom must be used as if it were designed primarily as an aid to the teacher in meeting the needs of each one of her students. Actually, only a few of these tools and their uses have been illustrated in this chapter. Each year, more and more firms will begin to introduce materials and furnishings which are more flexible and more creative than ever before. New dimensions will be added to the classroom to make the task of educating students for tomorrow easier and more effective.

SUMMARY

The need to individualize instruction so that the learning experience can be a successful undertaking for students is well-recognized today by most educators.

However, many have failed at wholly satisfying these needs because they have viewed individualization on a restricted plane. Individualization must be implemented in every area that has any effect whatsoever on the learning process — the school plant, furnishings, instructional materials and equipment, and, last but not least, there must be administrators and teachers who "think individualization" constantly.

8. DEVELOPING INDIVIDUAL STUDY UNITS

> *The best hope for curriculum continuity and for the instruction that recognizes the differences in pupils and allows them to proceed at their own learning rates lies in breaking the needless chains that exist through school grade level organizations.*
>
> *Morton Alpren*

If an administrator is to be successful in the implementation of the nongraded concept, he must be able to design and develop a curriculum from which effective individual study units may be constructed. This ability imbues teachers with a feeling of security and will encourage them to rely on the instructional format for individualizing the educational program. It is well to be aware at all times that habits formed in traditional education are deep rooted and very difficult to displace, both in parents and in educators. This factor makes the task of educating the student much more difficult, especially in view of the fact that we have lived with the ills of traditionalism for such a lengthy period of time. At this juncture, the author is reminded of the fact that the first public schools established by the Puritans in 1600 were charged with the heavy responsibility of deluding Satan in his quest for power over the minds of the young. Unfortunately, it would not be much amiss, if, today, traditional education were to be regarded as the Satan which despoils young minds. Nongraded education presents a method by which young minds may be expanded.

It is incumbent upon the professional staff of a school district which is initiating the nongraded concept to be thoroughly familiar with the basic procedures for planning and developing a superior curriculum from which individual study units will be constructed. The following prerequisites should be borne in mind for the development of individual study units:

Establishing the Role of the Curriculum Coordinator

The assistant superintendent in charge of instruction, or the director of curriculum and instruction has primary responsibility as chief curriculum coordinator for the school district. Through his leadership, resource persons within and outside the school district join in making concerted efforts to revise the present curriculum from traditionalism to nongradedness. Neagley and Evans convey quite effectively his responsibilities as follows:

1. To keep the chief school administrator informed on major thrusts and directions in curriculum development, through personal contact and through minutes of the curriculum council meetings

2. To chair the curriculum council, at least initially, and to guide its deliberations. He also sets up regular meetings of this important body.

3. To keep abreast as a generalist of the latest developments affecting the curriculum, such as the national educational laboratories, current legislation, the developing Educational Research Information Center, and other forces.

4. To work closely with the coordinators of elementary and secondary education in organizing the district program of curriculum evaluation and development. Regular weekly meetings should be scheduled and almost daily informal contacts encouraged.

5. To work with the K-12 subject area coordinators in examining the latest research and new curricula; to assist them in working with individual teachers and curriculum committees.

6. To maintain cooperative relationships with the intermediate unit office or the regional curriculum center, so that curriculum consultants and resource materials will be available when needed.

7. To prepare and justify the budget for curriculum development.

8. To be the chief school district representative with parents and community groups interested in the curriculum.

9. To organize with the chief librarian an extensive professional curriculum library and resource center.[1]

Forming a Curriculum Council

A nongraded curriculum council, which is organized by the administrator in charge of instruction, should be established so that involvement by personnel at the early childhood, elementary and secondary levels is included. An effort should be made to get maximum staff involvement. It is also advisable to invite parents and students to serve on the curriculum council. Teachers on the council should be utilized according to their abilities, interest, creativity, and experience. Because of the variance in aptitudes which will exist, some teachers will serve as researchers, or as planners, or as writers, or in various other categories.

As a rule, first year teachers should not be members of the council. They will need to utilize all of their precious time in adjusting to the daily routine of the school and the personalities of their students. All building principals should be ex-officio members of the council, since they will be the initiators of any curriculum change which is to take place. Although the specific number of members which is most effective to serve as a curriculum council is difficult to arrive at, if the size of the school is to be used as a determinant, the following may serve as a guide:

1. Two to four teachers per level;
2. Elementary and secondary coordinators;
3. Various supervisors, such as math, reading, science, etc,;
4. Two representatives from the Citizens' Advisory Council and two from the Student Council.

Teachers' Receptivity to Change

Some teachers are reluctant to accept change. Some don't like to be told to do anything; others will go along with the group; and some won't go along with anyone, regardless of what is presented to them. This variance in teacher attitudes must be taken into

---

[1] Ross L. Neagley and N. Dean Evans, *Handbook for Effective Curriculum Development* (Englewood Cliffs, N. J.: Prentice-Hall, Inc., 1967), pp. 133, 134.

consideration, particularly in terms of the composition of the curriculum committee, for it could well have an adverse effect on the committee's creativity and production. When forming the committee, only those teachers who have evidenced a receptivity to change should be asked to serve, and they should be chosen from among those who have a record of performing well in the classroom. Teachers who have been troublemakers, eccentrics, or conflict-laden are to be avoided and should not be assigned to the committee.

While teachers must be made to feel that they are calling the signals, the coordinator must be able to get the committee to act expeditiously in order to get activities started on the road to completion. If he does not, the committee may end up as one of those groups which do much talking and assembling, but accomplish little in the way of creative work.

An alternative problem which may occur was very well illustrated in one case where the coordinator was attempting to persuade the committee to set up a sub-committee of teachers to incorporate substance into a creative idea which originated with the chief school administrator. The teachers arbitrarily assumed that the coordinator was trying to impose the unilateral demands of the chief school administrator upon them and, as a result, they refused to act. In the end, the coordinator had to resort to political machinations to obtain a chairman and get a committee set up.

It is essential that those teachers selected to serve on committees be only those who are top-notch, creative, dedicated professionals. For example, one school district selected all team leaders to serve on the committee. Their only problem arose from the fact that they had more than 25 team leaders serving and, in actuality, this was much too large a committee. It is essential, too, to remember that these teachers must be allotted time away from their regular school duties to meet and give real importance to the committee.

Functions of the Curriculum Council

1. To recommend a policy on the curriculum and to assure that all curriculum development activities are properly coordinated.

2. To re-examine the philosophy of the school program to determine if revisions are necessary.

3. To examine the aims of the educational program and, where necessary, to make revisions therein.

4. To decide, in collaboration with building principals and staff, the major areas which are to be given priority.

5. To prepare lists of consultants and experts who are to aid in the development of curriculum and individual study units.

6. To identify and appoint various sub-committees that will be responsible for working in the various disciplines.

7. To keep all professional staff personnel informed about the activities of the curriculum council through minutes of meetings and curriculum bulletins.

8. To review Citizens' Advisory Council recommendations on curriculum.

9. To establish evaluation guidelines for determining strengths and weaknesses of the curriculum in order to make improvements.

The curriculum council should proceed at once to undertake extensive research and the collection of a massive fund of data pertaining to curriculum. This should include a perusal of every available publication which will keep them informed of new curriculum developments. In addition, the council should forward to nongraded schools questions about their planning and implementation procedures. It is of the utmost importance that all resource materials be stored in one center which is easily accessible to the professional staff members. Relevant books should be purchased and stored in a teachers' resource room. A bibliography section, which the reader may find useful, is appended to this volume.

The Curriculum Council Budget

In order to revise the present curriculum for nongradedness, the professional staff will be called upon to perform extra work for which they should receive extra remuneration. The following are examples of budget allocations for the curriculum council while it is developing the nongraded curriculum:

1. Funds should be allocated for 11th and 12th month salary differentials, so that teachers may work on improving or revising the curriculum during the summer months.

2. Funds should be allocated for the hiring of substitute teachers so that curriculum personnel will have ample opportunities to attend conferences, make visitations to successful innovative schools, and attend regular curriculum meetings.

3. Funds should be allocated for the retaining of substitute teachers or additional teachers, so that curriculum personnel will have time during the school day to work on the nongraded curriculum.

4. These funds should be supplemented by Federal and State funds, particularly, ESEA Title I and Title III.

Organizing Curriculum Sub-Committees

Each member of the council should be an initiator in terms of organizing various sub-committees. Sub-committees should be formed for all the various subject areas. After the sub-committees have been organized and oriented, development of individual study units should take place as described below:

Members of the staff should be asked to volunteer for the various sub-committees and, if possible, should be remunerated for their services. After all, since the tasks confronting these committees will be time-consuming and demanding, it is only reasonable that some remuneration be paid to teachers who are involved.

However, some administrators feel that the selection of teachers to serve on sub-committees should be left to their discretion. It is their view that only highly competent teachers should serve on these committees, and that more than anyone else, the administrators are qualified to determine this. In some instances, it may be necessary to retain full-time substitutes to replace regular teachers who must devote full-time services to the development of curriculum. The size of each sub-committee should be kept to a minimum to permit efficient, integrated planning and performance, but each sub-committee should also be large enough to function comfortably without the pressures of overburdening.

Developing the Organizational Chart

The first step to be undertaken is the development of a curriculum organization chart. The most effective organizational chart is comprised of two sections. The main section of the organizational chart lists the items of major importance while the secondary portion contains further detailing and delineations built upon the first section. For example, as can be seen by Figure 8-1 on page 144, one of the major headings on the organizational chart for reading would be "Developing Word Power," while the secondary section contains an elaboration of the steps to be taken to achieve word power.

Preparing Behavioral Objectives

Suitable efforts should then be made to establish a continuum of sequential behavioral objectives which are the basic requirements of the course. These objectives should be precisely delineated so that learning activities may be thoroughly organized, and learning may be guided by them. Tests which will truly evaluate should be constructed and administered.

An example of the behavioral objectives of the reading continuum follows:

1. Learning to use language to classify various experiences;
2. Using new words;
3. Adding to vocabulary through listening to stories;
4. Developing interest in words through picture dictionary;
5. Recognizing qualifying words for understanding situations;
6. Understanding the effects of varied intonations.

Constructing the Flow Chart

The next step to be undertaken is the creation of a curriculum flow chart, based upon the organization chart and the behavioral objectives, which will be a concise identification of the varied inner levels. In other words, the entire curriculum may be imposed on the flow chart, as is partially evidenced in Figure 8-2 on pages 145 and 146. An analogous thought which proves relevant in the preparation of nongraded curriculum and the development of individual study units is the structure of a tree. The roots of the tree represent the

ORGANIZATIONAL CHART
(Partial)

Developing Word Power	Getting and Interpreting Meaning	Developing Work-Study Skills
Expanding Speech Vocabulary	Getting the Main Thought	Following Directions
Developing Speech Vocabulary	Finding and Relating Details	Locating Information
Using Structured Analysis	Determining Sequence	Selection, Following, Recalling Information
	Drawing Inferences	Organizing Information
	Cultural Reading	Using Graphic Representation
		Mastering the Mechanics of Silent and Oral Reading

Figure 8-1. *Organizational chart (reading).*

FLOW CHART
(Partial)

SKILL I: Developing Word Power	SKILL II: Getting and Interpreting Meaning	SKILL III: Developing Word Study Skill
A. Expanding Oral Vocabulary	A. Getting the Main Thought	A. Following Instructions
Level B	**Level B**	**Level B**
(1) Learning to use language for experience clarification. Using new words in personal language patterns.	(1) Developing realization that a series of connected sentences refer to a single main thought.	(1) Following oral instructions given in uninterrupted sequence. Following simple instructions independently.
(2) Adding to vocabulary by listening to stories, retelling, dramatizing, etc.	**Level C**	**Level C**
(3) Developing interest in words, using picture dictionary.	(1) Developing the understanding that the main idea of a paragraph is usually contained in the first sentence (in materials read at this level).	(1) Gaining independence by following simple printed instructions contained in practice materials.
(4) Recognizing qualifying words (adjectives and adverbs) which add to understanding of situations.	**Level D**	**Level D**
(5) Exhibiting awareness of the effect of intonation variations on the meanings of words that are spoken or heard.	(1) Developing realization that the main idea may appear at the beginning, middle or end of a paragraph.	(1) Developing ability to observe specific patterns in following instructions.
		(1) Reading entire problem for general idea, rereading to note specific steps to be taken, carrying out steps. Rereading problem again to insure completion of problem.

Figure 8-2. *Flow chart (reading).*

Level C
(1) Exhibiting awareness of differences between out-of-school language.

(2) Increasing use of words heard on TV or radio.

(3) Continuing to add vocabulary and definitions using picture dictionary.

Level E
(1) Extending skills to printed materials in which the main thought is not lucidly expressed or is elaborated over several paragraphs.

Level F
(1) Ability to make generalizations on the basis of evaluating main ideas from several sources.

Level G
(1) Extending ability to make generalizations.

Level E
(1) Extending ability to independently follow specific written instructions.

Flow chart (reading) (cont'd).

foundation of the nongraded concept of education — the members of the curriculum council and sub-committees, their research, collection of materials, and actual performance on the curriculum committee. The trunk of the tree is represented by the organizational chart which, if the council has done an effective job, will constitute a massive, many-ringed trunk. The branches and leaves on the tree are represented by the flow chart, and the fruit of the tree is, of course, the superior individual study units.

Devising Recommendations for Acquiring Particular Skills Denoted on the Flow Chart

The following is a suggested chart of skills and procedures which might constitute objectives:

SKILL	*PROCEDURE*
1. Expanding oral vocabulary.	1(a) Verbalization of story by having student relate experience.
	Narration to students of stories on tape recorders and phonographs.
	Student assignments to bring in pictures which develop word interest.
	Student identification of descriptive words.
	Teacher recitation to demonstrate meaning of vocal inflections.
	Students' usage of words heard on radio and television.
	Technical appraisal of word usage when student recites a story.

SKILL	*PROCEDURE*
2. Developing a reading vocabulary.	Devising experience chart which relates to daily experience of child. The child should be capable of associating the oral symbols designated on this chart.

As above, with the addition of written words presented on printed matter. |

At this point, the committee may wish to pause and use the Flow Chart as a guide for the Skill-Level Sequences Curriculum Plan. If, however, the committee desires to go ahead, the next step is the formulation of individually prescribed units through the following suggested procedures:

Preparing Individual Study Units

There are 8 basic sections to the Individual Study Units, as illustrated in Figure 8-3 on page 149. These sections include the following:

1. Content Area. This describes the title of the unit, the skill or concept which is the subject of study, and the level.

2. Rationale. In this section, a statement of the purpose of the unit is presented which indicates what is to be studied, and why it is important for the student to learn the material in the particular unit.

3. Behavioral Objectives. This portion identifies the actual performance which the student should be able to make after he has successfully completed the unit. The condition is indicated, the expected act or performance is so stated, as well as the minimum standard required to demonstrate success.

4. Self- or Pre-Test. Either or both of these may be required. The Self-Test gives the student an opportunity to periodically assess his own progress. The Pre-Test is utilized to determine how much the student already knows about the subject under study in the particular unit.

5. Learning Experience. This section is an instructional narrative about the lesson which is oriented so that it is relevant to the realities of the student. Also included in this section are Learning Activity Options which permit the student to continue his Learning

INDIVIDUAL STUDY UNIT

Content:	Reading
Skill A:	Reciting words beginning with "b"
Level:	5
Rationale:	The purpose of this unit is to enable you to read words which begin with the letter "b", like "boat", so that you will be a better reader.
Behavioral Objective:	After you have completed this unit, you will be able to read and recite words which begin with "b" with 90% accuracy.
Self-Test:	Instruction: Put a circle around what you think is the correct word which goes in the empty space to complete the sentence:

1. John is a ____boy. (bad, had)
2. Mary put money in the ____. (bank, sank)
3. The pears are in the ____. (rag, bag)
4. The girls play ____. (call, ball)
5. John and Paul are ____. (toys, boys)

Learning Experience:	The teacher will direct the student to the table containing the Language Master and the file box in which the "b-sound" cards are contained. The student will then put all of these cards through the recorder in order to listen to the sounds.
Learning Activity Options:	Choose any one of the two options below to complete your learning experience:

1. Proceed to the tape bin and take out the "b" tapes. Go to the tape recorder located in one of the carrels and play the tape. When you finish listening to this tape, complete the Post-Test.

2. Proceed to the Du Kane Projector and view and listen to the sound filmstrip on "b" sounds. At the end of the filmstrip, complete the Post-Test.

Post-Test:	Put a circle around the word which you think belongs in the sentence:

1. I sleep in a ____. (red, bed)
2. We go home at the ____. (tell, bell)
3. Dick ____ the cookies. (bit, sit)
4. I like to sail in my ____. (boat, goat)
5. We have a new ____. (took, book)

Attitudinal Objective:	Did you like this Unit? Why?
Evaluation:	

Figure 8-3. *An individual study unit.*

Experience by selecting the manner and method in which he wishes to pursue his knowledge. In actuality, these Options constitute the "what" and "how" of the student's learning. When the student undertakes a unit, no more than 40% of these Options are required to be completed.

6. *Post-Test.* This test is given to the student to determine how well he has mastered the content of the unit. If he is unsuccessful, he is then re-cycled through the remaining Learning Activity Options.

7. Attitudinal Objectives. This section is included to determine the student's attitude about the particular unit, and also to broaden his perspectives concerning the material in the unit.

8. Evaluation. In this section, the teacher evaluates the student's completion of the unit, and prescribes subsequent units or Learning Activity Options for the student.

PAR Factors in Learning

In order to enhance the effectiveness of the Individual Study Units, the PAR factors of learning must be incorporated. These PAR factors can serve to increase opportunities for self-directed learning and, at the same time, bring essential relevance to the academic content to dispel attitudes of resentment. The PAR factors of learning consist of:

1. Programmed Learning in which the instructional program is carefully constructed to enable the student to proceed from one concept to another under his own impetus. Individual study units devised by students and teachers, together with programmed texts, will be utilized to support this factor.

2. Assimilated Learning which is permeating and pervasive, making the student feel that he is a part of the total experience. Commercially produced learning games will be supplemented by materials which have been created locally by students and teachers in order to support this factor.

3. Reality Learning in which the individual student is exposed to real situations which buttress the learning experience. Those areas are to be selected by teachers and students for visits which will provide the most realistic experience in the field of the subject being studied.

Establishing Inventory and Placement Tests

Inventory or Placement Tests should be devised in order to determine the appropriate placement level for individual students. In some instances, the following commercially prepared tests can serve this purpose:

1. Botel Reading Inventory, Grades 1-12
   Follett Publishing Co., 1010 W. Washington Blvd.,
   Chicago, Illinois

2. Diagnostic Reading Scales, Grades 1-8
   California Test Bureau, 206 Bridge Street,
   New Cumberland, Pennsylvania

3. Diagnostic Reading Tests, Grades K-4, 4-8, 7-13
   Committee on Diagnostic Reading Tests Inc.,
   Mountain Home, North Carolina

4. Group Diagnostic Reading Aptitude and
   Achievement Tests, Grades 3-9
   C. H. Nevins Printing Co.,
   811 Bryn Manor Island, Bayshore Gardens,
   Bradenton, Florida.

It is vitally important that all of the foregoing steps be completed before any attempts at construction of pre-tests and post-tests. After the inventory or placement tests have been prepared, pre-tests may also be used to re-test the student after he has successfully completed the post-test in a particular unit. The pre-test should be administered to the student whenever he is about to be placed on a new skill. The pre-tests should be constructed so as to test more items than are indicated on the placement or inventory test. In actuality, the post-test should be very similar to the pre-test, especially in terms of each skill to be included, for if a student achieves mastery of a particular skill indicated on the post-test, he is then permitted to proceed to the next skill. It is eminently advisable that pre-tests and post-tests be available, not only in written form, but also on audiotape, so that content placement for a student can be determined without complete reliance on his reading level. This is particularly important in the subject areas of science and social studies. When the tests are being devised by the staff, extreme caution should be taken to insure that the test bears a direct relationship to the particular skill.

Developing an Individual Study Unit Placement Form

This form usually contains the outline of the flow chart, as may be observed in Figure 8-4 on pages 152 and 153. At the top of the page, the name of the student, the teacher, the classroom, and also the particular skills are indicated. As can be noted, Skill I, Level B-1, is entitled "Expanding Oral Vocabulary." The Skill is "I," which is entitled "Developing Word Power." In order to expand his oral vocabulary at Level B-1, the student learns to use language to clarify experiences and uses new words in his own language patterns. The set of three skills are delineated as:

SKILL I	SKILL II	SKILL III
DEVELOPING WORD POWER	*GETTING AND INTERPRETING MEANING*	*DEVELOPING WORD STUDY*
Level B Expanding Oral Vocabulary 1 Learning to use language for experience clarification. Using new words in personal language patterns.	*Level B Getting the Essential Thought* 1 Developing realization that a series of connected sentences refer to a single main thought.	*Level B Following Instructions* 1 Following oral instructions given in uninterrupted sequence. Following simple instructions independently.
2 Adding to vocabulary by listening to stories, retelling, dramatizing, etc.	*Level C* 1 Developing the understanding that the main idea of a paragraph is usually contained in the first sentence (in materials read at this level).	*Level C* 1 Gaining independence by following simple printed instructions contained in practice materials.
3 Developing interest in words, using picture dictionary.		
4 Recognizing qualifying words (adjectives and adverbs) which add to understanding of situation.	*Level D* 1 Developing realization that the main idea may appear at the beginning, middle or end of a paragraph.	*Level D* 1 Developing ability to observe specific patterns in following directions. Reading entire problem for general idea, rereading to note specific steps to be taken, carrying out steps. Rereading problem again to insure completion of problem.
5 Exhibiting awareness of effect of intonation variations on the meanings of words that are spoken or heard.	*Level E* 1 Extending skills to printed materials in which the main thought is not lucidly expressed or is elaborated on in several paragraphs.	

Figure 8.4 Individual study unit placement form (reading)

Level C	Level F	Level E
1 Exhibiting awareness of differences in out-of-school language.	1 Ability to make generalizations on the basis of evaluating main ideas from several sources.	1 Extending ability to independently follow specific written instructions.
2 Increasing use of words heard on TV and radio.	Level G	
3 Continuing to add vocabulary and definitions, using picture dictionary	1 Extending ability to make generalizations.	

Individual study unit placement form (reading) (contd.)

1. Skill I – Developing Word Power
2. Skill II – Getting and Interpreting Meaning
3. Skill III – Developing Word Study Skill.

While this is a comprehensive chart on several skills and levels, some revisions, additions, or deletions may provide a more appropriate outline for various school districts.

If the sub-committee is going to develop the inventory test, it would be wise to include the test on the placement form. In this way, the student may be given the test which is then scored and entered on the placement form immediately. If, for example, a student was tested on three skills and did very well, this could be indicated by placing an appropriate reference in the box adjacent to the Skill Level 1, Level B-1. For illustrative purposes, let us say this score was 70 percent. Going on with further testing of this student, let us say that at Level B-2, he scored 85 percent correct; 95 percent correct at Level B-3; and 50 percent correct at Level B-4. On Skill 2, let us pretend that this student scored 87 percent correct at Level B-1; 80 percent correct at Level C-1; 70 percent correct at Level D, and 50 percent correct at Level E. Subsequently, on Skill 3, this imaginary student scored 85 percent correct at Level B-1; 85 percent correct at Level C-1; 90 percent correct at Level D-1, and 80 percent correct at Level E-1. This would indicate that any instruction now to be undertaken should begin at these three levels in the areas where our fictitious student scored less than 85 percent. Particularly in reading where testing rarely results in constant scores, it is important to consider these three measuring items. The next step which this teacher should take with our student is to give him a pre-test to determine where the actual deficiencies lie within that particular level which requires additional work. Only after these steps have been taken, and the pre-test evaluated, is it time to compose an individual study unit for this particular student pursuant to the information on the placement form and in the pre-test.

The basic criteria which must be kept in mind when implementing the nongraded concept with the introduction of individual study units are as follows:

1. Usually, a test should be administered to each student to determine the extent of weakness and strength in particular areas. These tests may be known as either placement or inventory tests.

2. Each student should receive his own individual unit and the teacher must be considered as a component of the unit.

3. Lucid directions should be given for the use of all supplemental textbooks, workbooks, and tools of educational technology.

4. At times, wherever and whenever it seems indicated, grouping procedures are recommended, i.e., independent study, small group instruction, or large group instruction.

5. Post-tests should be given to each student when he has completed a unit of study in order to determine exactly how much he has gained. Any pre-tests which are administered should be similar to post-tests.

6. All tests should be scored by teacher aides or machines, but evaluations should be made by the teacher.

7. Each student should be required to satisfactorily complete a minimum number of units in order to become eligible either to proceed to the next unit, or to graduate from school.

8. It should be emphasized that no two individual study units should be exactly alike. All factors must be individually appraised when preparing an individual study unit for a student. Most important among these factors are motivational drive, aspirational level, and level of interest. Therefore, although a specifically prescribed curriculum may be adhered to, the total package should differ according to the needs of the individual student.

SUMMARY

In order to accurately individualize the instructional program, individual study units should be developed and used by each student in a classroom. However, effective individual study units cannot be created unless certain preliminary steps are taken. Among these are the establishment of a curriculum council with various sub-committees, the development of a curriculum organization chart, and the construction of a flow chart. Of no lesser importance is the need to delineate with some specificity the procedures to be used in the acquisition of certain skills, and the need for valid pre-testing and post-testing for inventory and determination of mastery and placement. There should be a primary element of continuity between the curriculum, the organizational chart, the flow chart, the individual study units, the inventory or placement tests, pre- and post-tests, the reporting procedure to parents, and the students' cumulative progress report. It is satisfying to note that, among those schools boasting individualization of instruction, where these preliminaries have been adhered to the school has evolved a fine program which pays more than lip service to the concept of individualized instruction.

9. REPORTING PUPIL PROGRESS

TO PARENTS

Since the skills work expected of children in a nongraded class differs from one child to the next, there is no uniform standard similar to that in a graded school against which to rate the way children perform.

John L. Tewksbury

Administrators have long been perplexed over appropriate methods for depicting the academic progress of a student. Numerous methods have been devised by professional educators as suitable means by which parents might be informed, with clarity and brevity, of the progress of their children. Usually, in the kindergarten and sometimes in the first grade, parent-teacher conferences were considered by most schools to be the most feasible method. In subsequent grades, throughout the entire school career, numerical and alphabetical indications were used by most schools at varying periods of time in the history of public school education. At certain periods the use of one of these indications was more predominant than the other. Private schools generally preferred numerical rather than alphabetical indicators. At most higher institutions of learning, educators have added to the other indications of progress the greatly simplified "pass" or "fail" notation. The latter plan has been the subject of some criticism because it is not accepted by all universities and because it fails to adequately evaluate quality or progress. Somewhere along the way, educators lost sight of the primary purposes of establishing a system of grades, i.e., to evaluate academic progress of students. Most grading systems tended to deteriorate into a practice of simply "marking" students, rather than "evaluating" their progress. After many attempts to devise an adequate reporting system for parents and more than 100 years of experience at it, educators managed only to evolve a grading system which demonstrated amassing of subject matter and refrained, almost as if on purpose, from giving any true indication of pupil progress. Unfortunate though it is, in actuality the traditional grading system has been constructed around a concept of failure, since a student who does not come up to a certain numerical or alphabetical standard is automatically failed, even though he may have made some progress in failing! It is incomprehensible that this traditional grading system has lasted as long as it has, especially when one considers the critical inequities in a system which denotes a child as failing simply because he has received "69" instead of "70," and then demands of him another year of studying the same subject from the self-same texts. Perhaps the largest deficiency within the traditional grading system is the fact that it makes no allowance for the wide range of pupil talents, abilities, and interest levels. Obviously, the traditional grading system has no place in a nongraded program which places stress on individualized instruction permitting individual progress.

Developing the Nongraded Progress Report Card

There are several basic principles which should be observed when developing a nongraded progress report card that will evaluate individual progress with clarity. Among these principles are:

1. The objectives of the teacher and the school should be borne in mind when devising an appropriate report form, because progress and development in terms of performance can be judged only after continuous study of the student's record in conjunction with these characteristics and objectives.

2. There should be conformity in the terms and symbols used, and effort should be made to insure correct translation of these terms and symbols by all who will be reading the report. Only in this way can the report have any significance in terms of depicting the student's behavior.

3. Attempts should be made to avoid the use of any terms which might be interpreted in vastly different ways by different types of people.

4. The positive performances and characteristics which are usually a part of the nongraded program should be clearly interpreted. In the rare instances where no progress is made, it might be wise to prepare a special report which should be the subject of personal conferences to determine why a student shows no progress. Too often, reports tend to emphasize negative factors in student performance.

5. It is important that the progressive report card contain the following information:

>A. Student academic progress according to his own abilities.

>B. Quality of student performance.

>C. Teacher evaluation of effort on the part of the student.

6. Realistic information should be requested in terms of the behavior that teachers are most likely to observe in order to make a qualified judgment. If these are brief, but in depth, it becomes more possible for teachers to indicate some evidence for all the items.

7. Any increased workload to administrators, teachers, or clerical employees by virtue of the intricacy of a reporting form should be carefully evaluated and, wherever possible, should be avoided.

8. The format used should be relatively simple in design in order to effectively communicate individual progress to the student, his parents, and others.

9. No report should give the impression that a static level of ability has been predetermined and that students must always achieve at that level.

10. Skills should be identified and described on the Progress Report Card along a continuum.

Recommended Reporting Methods

The methods of reporting to parents which are described in this chapter were recommended after reviewing hundreds of reporting methods used in nongraded schools and after conferences with numerous nongraded educational consultants. These methods, however, are only suggested as guides, and any reporting procedure remains, as is the nongraded educational program, a matter of personal choice as best for the school involved.

There are two basic methods of reporting to parents, the progress report card and the conference. Neither method of reporting to parents is going to be more effective than the other. Each one offers some element that the other does not, i.e., gaining useful information from parents, personally apprising parents of weaknesses and strength, and providing written commentary on individual progress.

The Progress Report Card

Basically, there are two types of nongraded progress report cards, the graph method and the chart method.

The Graph Method

The graph method provides a truly contemporary approach to reporting to parents. This report form quickly provides the parent with a visual picture of the student's achievement, the relative value of such achievement, and any future remedy which may be undertaken for cure. The Graph Progress Report Card is a bar graph representation of skill concepts or levels of the curriculum showing progress along a continuum. There are usually two basic sections for which provision should be made:

1. Section I is the title page containing information about the school, the name of the student and his teacher, the school year, the homeroom number, attendance, and pertinent explanatory material about the reporting system. In this section, space is sometimes allocated for parental signature.

2. Section II is the evaluative section where the progress of the student is evaluated objectively in terms of student performance and subjectively in terms of teacher judgment of student performance. This area should also include the name of the student, his subject area and school year. Also included in this section is the following information:

A. The content area contains identification of skills, units, or levels enumerated on the progress report card.

B. The bar graph area which may be either horizontally adjacent to the content section or diagonally adjacent to the content section should contain an identification of the marking period and progress report on the student's achievement.

C. The teacher's judgment area is usually located near the bottom of the form, giving a subjective evaluation of how much effort the teacher feels is being put forth.

Nongraded Progress Report Card — A Reality!

It was the efforts of a select group of Colorado teachers and administrators who, along with Dr. Glenn Nimnicht of Colorado State College, spent a week during 1964 at the Seventh Annual Small Schools Workshop at Vail, Colorado, that resulted in a nongraded progress report card. An example of this report is illustrated on pages 173 and 174.[1]

The title page of the Graph Method is illustrated in Figure 9-1, page 164. Example I (Figure 9-2, page 165) illustrates a report form for a student who learns slowly and ended the last year achieving below the local norm. Although his progress in the first grading period is less than that expected for an average student, his progress is satisfactory for his capabilities and his teacher therefore shades progress as "Satisfactory" and, in the "Teacher's Judgment of Progress" box, checks "I am satisfied." During the second grading period, although the student makes just about the same progress, the quality of his work improves, so the teacher shades progress as "Very good" and checks "I am satisfied" in her judgment of progress. While progress is slower and of only satisfactory quality during the third grading period, as the teacher shows by shading less progress under "Satisfactory" and checking "could make more progress" in her judgment of progress, the fourth grading period is about the same as the first grading period.

---

[1] From a report published by Western States Small Schools Project for Colorado and the Colorado Department of Education; Paul Nachtigal, editor. The report was completed under a grant to the Colorado Department of Education, Byron W. Hansford, Commissioner, by the Ford Foundation.

Example II (Figure 9-3, page 166) illustrates a report form for a student of average capabilities who starts a little below average according to the local norm, but who finishes the first six weeks on a level with the local norm. During the second period, while the student does the expected amount of work the quality lessens somewhat, but during the third period it improves, although progress is slower. During the fourth quarter, he completes more work while retaining the quality of the preceding period, and continues doing average work according to the local norm through the fifth and sixth grading periods, so that he ends the year in readiness for the next level with the teacher's judgment of progress reflected by a checkmark in the "I am satisfied" area.

Example III (Figure 9-4, page 167) shows the progress of a student with higher than average capabilities who starts the year well-advanced. During the first grading period, progress for this student is not as fast as his capabilities would indicate, but is good according to the usual standards, as indicated by the teacher's report. During the second period progress is better, yet quality still needs improvement and, during the third grading period, work quality is better and the teacher feels progress is consistent with the student's potential. The level of achievement for this student continues upward for the remainder of the year.

Advantages and Disadvantages of the Graph Method

An advantage of this reporting method is that highly individualized and periodic progress is shown for the pupil by reference to terms such as "excellent," "very good" and "satisfactory." Among other advantages are:

1. Parents are informed of the skill with which the child is progressing.
2. Rate and amount of progress is immediately visible.
3. This method is comprehensive in scope and design.
4. This form of reporting is particularly useful in a nongraded high school.

However, there are disadvantages, among them·

1. The indication of "Local norms" and "National norms" which should not be included since, as mentioned before, they allow for the detrimental practice of comparing an individual child with other children.

2. Success in reporting to parents by this method is doubtful, unless care is exercised in a thorough explanation of the varied meanings of the card.

3. The comprehensiveness of this reporting procedure makes it difficult to plan.

4. In order to use this method of reporting with a high degree of competency, some teachers must attend intensive workshop sessions.

5. This reporting procedure might prove prohibitive in view of the fact that a different graph would be required for each subject area.

6. The graph might prove difficult to understand for those parents, students, and teachers not oriented to reading graphs.

An IPI Report Chart

An example of a sample report card which was designed by a committee of teachers, principals, and the author is illustrated in Figures 9-5 to 9-8. This reporting form was designed to depict graphically the progress of pupils studying mathematics under the Individually Prescribed Instruction program. This particular report form is unique because it is the first time an attempt has been made to get an evaluative opinion from all parties concerned with the student's education – the teacher, the parent and the student. The student is first given the opportunity to evaluate his own performance. This is done before the teacher's evaluation is inserted in order to avoid any subjective influence which the teacher's evaluation may exert on the student's opinion of his performance and progress. The teacher then evaluates the student's performance in school. Finally, the parent has an opportunity to indicate on the reporting form whether, in his opinion, the student is performing and progressing satisfactorily. The illustrated report form is contemporary and includes all the features which should be part of a report of pupil progress in a nongraded class.

The Chart Method

The Chart Progress Report Card is more frequently used than the Graph Progress Report Card, and this may be the reason why

Continuous Progress School
School Year 19___ -19___

Student_____   Teacher _____

Year in School _____   Room _____

Attendance

	(1st 6 Wk)	(2nd 6 Wk)	(3rd 6 Wk)	(4th 6 Wk)	(5th 6 Wk)	(6th 6 Wk)
Days Absent						
Times Tardy						

In our continous progress school, instruction and organization are designed to allow the student to move steadily forward at the maximum rate for his own ability. At the same time we want you to know how your child is achieving in relation to acceptable standards of comparison. On this report of student achievement, progress is shown in various ways.

1.   The quality of performance is shown by indicating achievement levels in the appropriate column for quality: Excellent, Very Good or Satisfactory. Continuous progress, however slowly achieved, does not permit failure in the ordinary sense, as a student does not progress to a higher level until he has satisfactorily completed the preceding task.

2.   Student progress through the curriculm is shown by recording movement upward along the graph. This is shown in comparison with what is expected of the average child in this school (local norms) and with other standards as shown in the lower column.

3.   When there has been no progress this will be indicated in the report. A complete absence of progress may be due to one of several causes and warrants a conference with the teacher.

4.   Quality and quantity of progress, unless otherwise indicated, are based on teacher judgment, as is the evaluation of student effort.

Two special notes to the parents:

1.   The description of progress are related to our continuous progress mathematics curriculm. Concepts adopted from Middletown Non-Graded Program, Middletown, R.I.

2.   Since we have a kindergarten in this district, it is counted as the child's first year in school; therefore, the average child would be doing seventh grade work in his eighth year of school.

Figure 9-1. *The graph method – title page.*

EXAMPLE I

REPORT FORM

SUBJECT___MATH___ STUDENT___A___

YEAR___19-___

CONCEPTS, SKILLS, KNOWLEDGE.

8. Plane figures _____

7. Measurement _____

6. Principles of non-metric geometry_____

5 Percent, percentage_____

4. Positive rational numbers-
      decimals_____

3 Positive rational numbers-
      fractions_____

2. Natural numbers
     and zero _____

1. Place value in our
     number system ____

MARKING PERIOD
Excellent
Very Good
Satisfactory
Local Norm
National Norm

1 2 3 4 5 6

6.0 6.5 7.0 7.5 8.0 8.5

GRADING PERIOD	1	2	3	4	5	6
I am satisfied	✓	✓			✓	✓
Could make more progress			✓	✓		
Quality of work needs to be improved						
We need a parent-teacher conference						

Figure 9-2. *The graph method – evaluative section – Example I.*

EXAMPLE II

REPORT FORM

SUBJECT___MATH___ STUDENT___B___

YEAR___19-___

CONCEPTS, SKILLS, KNOWLEDGE.

8. Plane figures _____

7. Measurement _____

6. Principles of non-metric geometry_____

5. Percent, percentage_____

4. Positive rational numbers–
   decimals_____

3. Positive rational numbers–
   fractions_____

2. Natural numbers
   and zero _____

1. Place value in our
   number system_____

MARKING PERIOD

Excellent
Very Good
Satisfactory
Local Norm
National Norm

6.0 6.5 7.0 7.5 8.0 8.5

GRADING PERIOD	1	2	3	4	5	6
I am satisfied	✓		✓	✓	✓	✓
Could make more progress						
Quality of work needs to be improved		✓				
We need a parent– teacher conference						

Figure 9-3. *The graph method – evaluative section – Example II.*

EXAMPLE III
REPORT FORM

SUBJECT____MATH____ STUDENT___C___

YEAR__19-__

CONCEPTS, SKILLS, KNOWLEDGE.

Plane figures

Measurement

Principles of non-metric geometry

Percent, percentage

Positive rational numbers—
decimals

Positive rational numbers—
fractions

Natural numbers
and zero

Place value in our
number system

MARKING PERIOD
Excellent
Very Good
Satisfactory
Local Norm
National Norm

GRADING PERIOD	1	2	3	4	5	6
I am satisfied			✓	✓		
Could make more progress					✓	✓
Quality of work needs to be improved	✓	✓				
We need a parent-teacher conference						

Figure 9-4. *The graph method – evaluative section – Example III.*

WYANDANCH PUBLIC SCHOOLS

INDIVIDUALLY PRESCRIBED INSTRUCTION

– MATHEMATICS –

REPORT FORM

Student...

Teacher...

Year ....

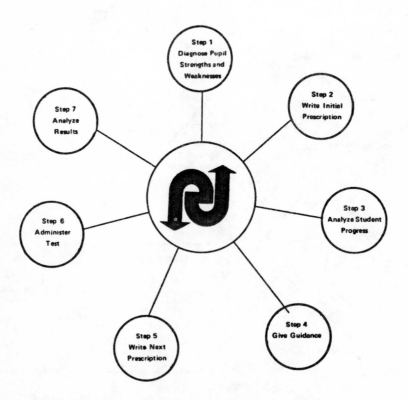

Figure 9-5. *An IPI progress report card – title page.*

PUPIL PROGRESS REPORT

HOW TO READ THE PROGRESS REPORT CARD
FOR INDIVIDUALLY PRESCRIBED INSTRUCTION

In IPI, the plan of instruction has been designed and organized to permit each student to progress at his max imum rate of speed, according to his individual abilities and his interest level The Progress Report Card has not been created to simply give your child a "grade" or a "mark" which does not really tell you anything about your child's actual progress, his strong points, or his weak ones This Progress Report is meant to give you a true evaluation of your child's academic progress in the particular subject area Student achievement is in dicated as follows

1 On the Pupil Progress Report graph, your child's progress is shown by recording his achievement in a particular skill across the chart from beginning level "A" to the more advanced level "H". The red color on the graph indicates the skill level at which your child started out. The green color indicates his progress during the period September thru January. The blue color indicates his progress from February through June.

2. A unique feature of this Progress Report is shown on the portion entitled "Teacher, Student and Parent Evaluation of Progress." In this area, your child's teacher evaluates the progress she believes he is making and the quality of the work he is performing In addition, space is provided for you, as a parent, to indicate to the school your evaluation of your child's progress and the quality of his performance. Finally, we ask your child to evaluate himself so that we may have some idea of how he feels he is progressing in school

If you have any question at all about your child's Progress Report, please do not hesitate to contact your child's principal

Figure 9-6. *An IPI progress report card – informative section.*

WYANDANCH PUBLIC SCHOOLS

INDIVIDUALLY PRESCRIBED INSTRUCTION

– MATHEMATICS –

PUPIL PROGRESS REPORT

MATHEMATICS SKILLS	LEVELS							
	A	B	C	D	E	F	G	H
NUMERATION								
PLACE VALUE								
ADDITION								
SUBTRACTION								
ADDITION / SUBTRACTION								
MULTIPLICATION								
DIVISION								
COMBINATION OF PROCESSES								
FRACTIONS								
MONEY								
TIME								
SYSTEMS OF MEASUREMENT								
GEOMETRY								
S. T.								

CODE:

COLOR RED – Indicates your child's original placement in each area.

COLOR GREEN – Indicates your child's progress in each area during the period from September through January.

COLOR BLUE – Indicates your child's progress in each area during the period from February through June.

Figure 9-7. *An IPI progress report card – evaluative section.*

WYANDANCH PUBLIC SCHOOLS

INDIVIDUALLY PRESCRIBED INSTRUCTION
– MATHEMATICS –
PUPIL PROGRESS REPORT

TEACHER, STUDENT, AND PARENT EVALUATION OF PROGRESS

TEACHER EVALUATION JANUARY	TEACHER EVALUATION JUNE
Check One	Check One
Progress is satisfactory _____	Progress is satisfactory _____
Progress could be better _____	Progress could be better _____
Check One	Check One
Quality of work is satisfactory _____	Quality of work is satisfactory. _____
Quality of work needs improvement _____	Quality of work needs improvement_____
COMMENTS_____	COMMENTS_____

STUDENT EVALUATION JANUARY	STUDENT EVALUATION JUNE
Check One	Check One
I think my progress is satisfactory _____	I think my progress is satisfactory _____
I can make better progress _____	I can make better progress _____
Check One	Check One
I am satisfied with the quality of my work _____	I am satisfied with the quality of my work _____
I think the quality of my work needs improvement _____	I think the quality of my work needs improvement _____
COMMENTS _____	COMMENTS:_____
Student's Signature _____	Student's Signature _____

PARENT EVALUATION JANUARY	PARENT EVALUATION JUNE
Check One	Check One
I think my child's progress is satisfactory _____	I think my child's progress is satisfactory _____
My child can make better progress _____	My child can make better progress _____
Check One	Check One
The quality of my child's work is satisfactory _____	The quality of my child's work is satisfactory _____
The quality of my child's work needs improvement _____	The quality of my child's work needs improvement _____
COMMENTS _____	COMMENTS _____
Parent's Signature _____	Parent's Signature _____

Figure 9-8. *An IPI progress report card – evaluative section.*

reporting to parents has been one of the major problems confronting the early initiators of the nongraded concept. This report card is similar in certain respects to the traditional report card and it might be said that the only basic difference lies in the fact that the Chart Progress Report Card is more detailed.

The Chart Progress Report Card is exactly what the name implies. It is a chart which indicates the academic progress of students. As does the graph method, this chart report card usually contains two basic sections:

1. Section I is composed of a title page containing basic information about the school, the name of the student and his teacher, the school year, location of assigned homeroom, attendance entry, and explanation of the reporting method.

2. Section II consists of the evaluative section and, if necessary, may be several pages in length. A heading should be included in this section which identifies the student, the section number, course area, and particular school year. Other sections which should be included in the evaluative section are:

A. Coded or key area which provides an explanation of the symbols used on the chart

B. Content area with descriptions of skills and concepts of levels, together with an explanation of how the chart is to be interpreted.

C. Teacher judgment area providing a subjective assessment by the teacher of the student's efforts, with appropriate comments.

D. Signature area for parents with space for any comments they might care to include.

When considering the use of the Chart Progress Report Card, it is important to remember the essential uniqueness of the nongraded system which predicates a special form of reporting far removed from that used in a graded system where all pupils are expected to master well-defined material confined to that grade. In the thoroughly nongraded system where each pupil progresses according to his own ability with individually geared textbooks and instruction, there is no single standard by which all children may be judged. In consideration of the nongraded concept, the sample chart method illustrated on Figures 9-9 and 9-10 conveys three different kinds of

REPORT FORM — PRIMARY UNIT

Bard Elementary School

School year (*1967*/*1968*)

(*Jack Smith*) is in his (*second*) year of the continuous progress primary unit. This program begins with kindergarten and continues until the child enters fourth grade. Each child is helped to work at the level where he is and to make as much progress as possible. This report form has been especially designed for use in a continuous progress program.

Every child is marked in each subject three times a year. Instead of receiving a single mark in a subject, three are given. These are entered in the boxes at the top of each page.

The teacher will schedule a conference with each child's parents once a year in October. Other conferences may be arranged if desired.

READING, ARITHMETIC, SPELLING, AND HANDWRITING

In these skill subjects, each child is encouraged to progress at his own rate through a series of tasks or levels. Different children in the same classroom will be working at different levels — some will do their work in greater depth than others.

Children who are progressing more slowly may need to spend extra time in the primary unit. Parents will be fully informed of such a need.

Figure 9-9. *The chart method — title page.*

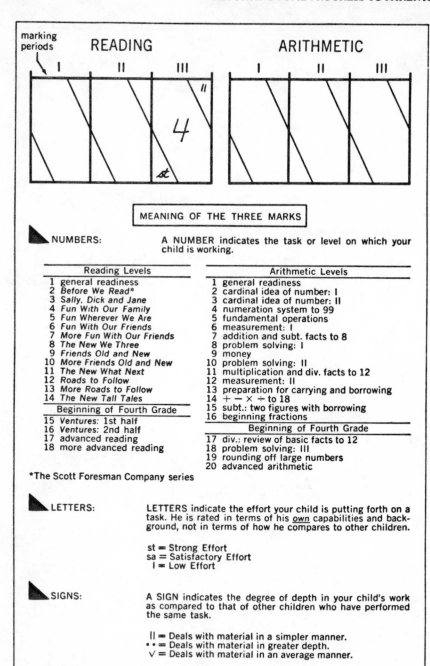

marking periods

READING

I   II   III

ARITHMETIC

I   II   III

| MEANING OF THE THREE MARKS |

NUMBERS: A NUMBER indicates the task or level on which your child is working.

Reading Levels	Arithmetic Levels
1 general readiness	1 general readiness
2 *Before We Read*＊	2 cardinal idea of number: I
3 *Sally, Dick and Jane*	3 cardinal idea of number: II
4 *Fun With Our Family*	4 numeration system to 99
5 *Fun Wherever We Are*	5 fundamental operations
6 *Fun With Our Friends*	6 measurement: I
7 *More Fun With Our Friends*	7 addition and subt. facts to 8
8 *The New We Three*	8 problem solving: I
9 *Friends Old and New*	9 money
10 *More Friends Old and New*	10 problem solving: II
11 *The New What Next*	11 multiplication and div. facts to 12
12 *Roads to Follow*	12 measurement: II
13 *More Roads to Follow*	13 preparation for carrying and borrowing
14 *The New Tall Tales*	14 $+ - \times \div$ to 18

Beginning of Fourth Grade	15 subt.: two figures with borrowing
15 *Ventures:* 1st half	16 beginning fractions
16 *Ventures:* 2nd half	Beginning of Fourth Grade
17 advanced reading	17 div.: review of basic facts to 12
18 more advanced reading	18 problem solving: III
	19 rounding off large numbers
	20 advanced arithmetic

＊The Scott Foresman Company series

LETTERS: LETTERS indicate the effort your child is putting forth on a task. He is rated in terms of his <u>own</u> capabilities and background, not in terms of how he compares to other children.

st = Strong Effort
sa = Satisfactory Effort
l = Low Effort

SIGNS: A SIGN indicates the degree of depth in your child's work as compared to that of other children who have performed the same task.

ll = Deals with material in a simpler manner.
• • = Deals with material in greater depth.
∨ = Deals with material in an average manner.

Figure 9-10. *The chart method – evaluative section.*

information about the child's progress; i.e., at what level is he working? How is his performance at this level? How much effort is he putting forth at this level? All of these features are considered in the context of comparing the individual child with his own capabilities and not with those of other students.

"General Readiness" in reading consists of the child's acquisition of various skills necessary to read the first primer, such as the ability to convey thoughts orally with correct language; to visually detect similarities and dissimilarities; and to master and perform formalized procedures of pre-reading skills. This reporting form provides 18 levels through which a child may progress in a nongraded class, the last four of which contain material which would have been offered only in the fourth and fifth grades of a graded system. In this sample, the names of the basal readers have been used to identify the level; however, specific reading skills might be listed instead. In the latter case, more room would have to be provided on the reporting form for more detailed information. There is sometimes a drawback, however, in providing too much information because of the difficulty involved in integrating all of it for a sound interpretation by parents.

As is illustrated in Figures 9-11* and 9-12*, which follow, the method of reporting pupil progress used by the Duluth Public Schools is both comprehensive and efficient. The Report of Pupil Progress (Figure 9-11) is submitted to parents together with a computerized summary on the Individual Student Progress Report (Figure 9-12). This latter provides an individualized, comprehensive, informative guide to tell a parent exactly what the student has undertaken, how he has progressed, what methods were used to teach him, and a clear and concise statement of what the student may be expected to know. The need for further concentration in a particular area is presented to the parent in a way that is meaningful and easily understood. The computerized summary which the Individual Student Progress Report presents might well be used to enhance the graph method of reporting, and also serve as an aid to the effectiveness of the conference reporting method.

---

*Reprinted by permission of The Board of Education of the City of Duluth, Minnesota.

Chester Park School   Date _____
William C. Simmons, Principal   Home Area _____

Report of Pupil Progress

Name _____ Grade _____

Curriculum	Teacher	I Performance as compared to the class as a whole			II Performance in relation to child's ability		
		Low	Average	High	Low	Average	High
Language Arts	J. Brieske						
Mathematics	A. Van Nevel						
Social Studies	D. Koch						
Science	J. Baird						
Physical Education	L. Ruppel						
Music	A. Green						
Art	C. Hansen						

Note: In any area of section II where the child is marked "Low" in terms of performance in relation to child's ability, the teachers will arrange a conference with the parents. The purpose will be to discuss how teacher(s) and parents can cooperate to help improve the child's performance in school.

In General, the child:	As Compared to Class as a Whole		
	Low	Average	High
Takes care of materials in a responsible manner			
Respects rights of others			
Exercises good self-control			
Makes good use of time			

Attendance: Present _____ Tardy _____
                   Absent _____

Additional Comments:

Parent's Comments: (If a conference is desired, please check here _____.)

Parent's Signature: _____

Figure 9-11. *Report of pupil progress.*

BOARD OF EDUCATION

DULUTH PUBLIC SCHOOLS   DULUTH, MINNESOTA

L V RASMUSSEN
SUPERINTENDENT

INDIVIDUAL STUDENT PROGRESS REPORT

PERIOD ENDING

NETTLETON SCHOOL – J. COWNS – PRINCIPAL

4-5-68

782730 CROSBY, RUTH M   ROOM   209   GRADE 6

10-6- 26
GIVEN A VARIETY CF SENTENCES WITH ERRORS IN THE USAGE CF WORDS, THE STU-
DENT WILL IDENTIFY THE ERRORS BY UNDERLINING EACH ERROR AND CORRECTING
IT IN THE SPACE ABOVE IT.
MINIMUM ACCEPTABLE 80

RESOURCES USED   ATTITUDE-2   ACCURACY-88

10-6- 37
GIVEN A NEWSPAPER AND A SHEET OF PAPER WITH THE COMPONENTS OF A NEWS-
PAPER LISTED ON IT, THE STUDENT WILL POINT OUT EACH PART –HEADLINE,
EDITORIAL, ETC.- AND WRITE A REASON FOR HAVING EACH PART IN A NEWSPAPER
ON THE SHEET PROVIDED.
MINIMUM ACCEPTABLE 80

RESOURCES USED FS   SRA   WS   ATTITUDE-1   ACCURACY-99

30-6- 55
GIVEN AN OUTLINE MAP OF BRAZIL AND THE GUINANAS WITH LISTED INFORMATION
DESCRIBING LAND USE, THE STUDENT IS ABLE TO READ THE MAP AND USE THE DATA
TO MAKE TRUE STATEMENTS OF THE OPEN SENTENCES PROVIDED.
MINIMUM ACCEPTABLE 80

RESOURCES USED TXT   ATTITUDE-2   ACCURACY-70

30-6- 55
GIVEN AN OUTLINE MAP OF BRAZIL AND THE GUINANAS WITH LISTED INFORMATION
DESCRIBING LAND USE, THE STUDENT IS ABLE TO READ THE MAP AND USE THE DATA
TO MAKE TRUE STATEMENTS OF THE OPEN SENTENCES PROVIDED.
MINIMUM ACCEPTABLE 80

RESOURCES USED TXT   ATTITUDE-2   ACCURACY-99

30-6- 58
GIVEN AN OUTLINE MAP OR MAPS OF LATIN AMERICA SHOWING THE CHIEF EXPORTS
AND AVERAGE INCOME FOR EACH COUNTRY, THE STUDENT IS ABLE TO USE THE DATA
TO MAKE TRUE STATEMENTS FOR EACH OF THE OPEN SENTENCES PROVIDED.
MINIMUM ACCEPTABLE 80

RESOURCES USED WS   ATTITUDE-2   ACCURACY-99

GENERAL RESOURCE CODING		ATTITUDE CODING
1 FILMSTRIP OR SLIDES-------------FS	7 TEACHING MACHINES-------------TM	1 - EXCELLENT
2 FILM (SOUND)------------------FAV	8 TEXTBOOK ------------------TEXT	2 - VERY GOOD
3 TAPE OR RECORDS---------------AUD	9 PROGRAMMED MATERIALS ----------PM	3 - GOOD
4 SRA AND OTHER LABS------------SRA	10 TAPE/FILMSTRIP OR TAPE SLIDE-- ----TFA	4 - POOR
5 WORKSHEET OR WORKBOOK ----------WS	11 TEACHER LED PRESENTATION --------TLP	5 - UNSATISFACTORY
6 MANIPULATIVE MATERIAL -----------MM	12 FILM (SILENT)-----------------FV	

Figure 9-12. *Individual student progress report.*

Advantages and Disadvantages of the Chart Method

The primary advantage of the chart method of reporting lies in the facility with which it may be constructed and comprehended. In addition, the chart reporting procedure:

1. Is useful in the nongraded primary and intermediate schools;
2. Does not require extensive teacher preparation in order for competency in its use to be acquired.

Among the numerous disadvantages are:

1. Levels are identified by basal texts.
2. Grade level is designated on report cards.
3. Progress is not visible as in the graph method, so that it is impossible to gauge steady progress.
4. It could be difficult for parents who are not accustomed to translating charts.

Graded Report Card vs. Nongraded Report Card

A glance at the following comparison chart will reveal the essential differences between the traditional graded report card and the contemporary nongraded report card:

Graded Report Card	*Nongraded Report Card*
1. The concept of failure is built into the educational program.	1. No child "fails" to progress, and so does not fail per se, but is permitted to achieve according to his own capabilities.
2. It is group oriented and subjectively based on what is, after all, the teacher's judgment.	2. It is individually oriented and, wherever possible, objectively based on individual achievement.

Graded Report Card	*Nongraded Report Card*
3. Progress is usually rated according to a standardized norm which the entire class is expected to achieve.	3. Progress is indicated by evaluating the student's individual progress in relation to his abilities.
4. Progress is evidenced by grades from one grading period to another.	4. Progress by a graph method is plotted along the line of a continuum to indicate progressive performance at each level of the student's academic growth.
5. It is designed to equate the individual student with the mass.	5. It is designed for equating the individual child with himself, his own abilities, his own talents and his own interest levels.
6. Evaluation is indicated by grades which are usually based on norms.	6. Evaluation is accomplished on the basis of each student's abilities, needs and interests.
7. Reports tend to favor the so-called "bright" and "gifted" child.	7. Reports tend to favor the so-called "underachiever" or "slow" learner.
8. It tends to be merely a "marking system."	8. It tends to be a true instrument of evaluation.
9. Subject areas are usually designated on the report.	9. Concepts, skills, or units of subject matter are usually designated on the report.

Cumulative Records

Figure 9-13 on page 181 illustrates a cumulative record using the graph method of reporting to parents. If we were to plot the student's progress over a period of years on this cumulative record, we would have a graphic representation of continuous progress in a nongraded program over several years. As is obvious, the cumulative record provides for the same indications of quality and quantity of progress as do the report forms which are restricted to a year of study, but allows for a graphical overview of a student's performance throughout a number of years of study.

Conference Method

The conference method of reporting to parents is excellent because it provides person-to-person contact, and it is particularly effective when the student is included in the conference, which, under normal circumstances, should last for approximately 15 or 20 minutes. Possibly there should be two types of conferences used in the procedure of reporting to parents:

A. Parent-Teacher Conferences

B. Parent-Teacher-Student Conferences

Hospitality, tact, graciousness, and diplomacy should all be keynotes in the parent-teacher conference. An effective method of beginning the conference and establishing an appropriate atmosphere for discussion of a student's progress is to have available work samples which illustrate the student's skills, talents, and interests, to be accompanied by an explanation from the teacher. However, teacher comments should never constitute the content of the entire conference. The parent should be encouraged and allowed to participate fully in the conference expressing worries, suggestions, and complaints, during all of which the teacher should avoid aggressive, "hard sell" tactics and attempt to lead the discussion with logic and persuasion, toward a goal of mutual agreement. The parent should be advised of his child's behavior at school and, where possible, a teacher may make constructive suggestions which should be considered, with alternative possibilities, by both teacher and parent.

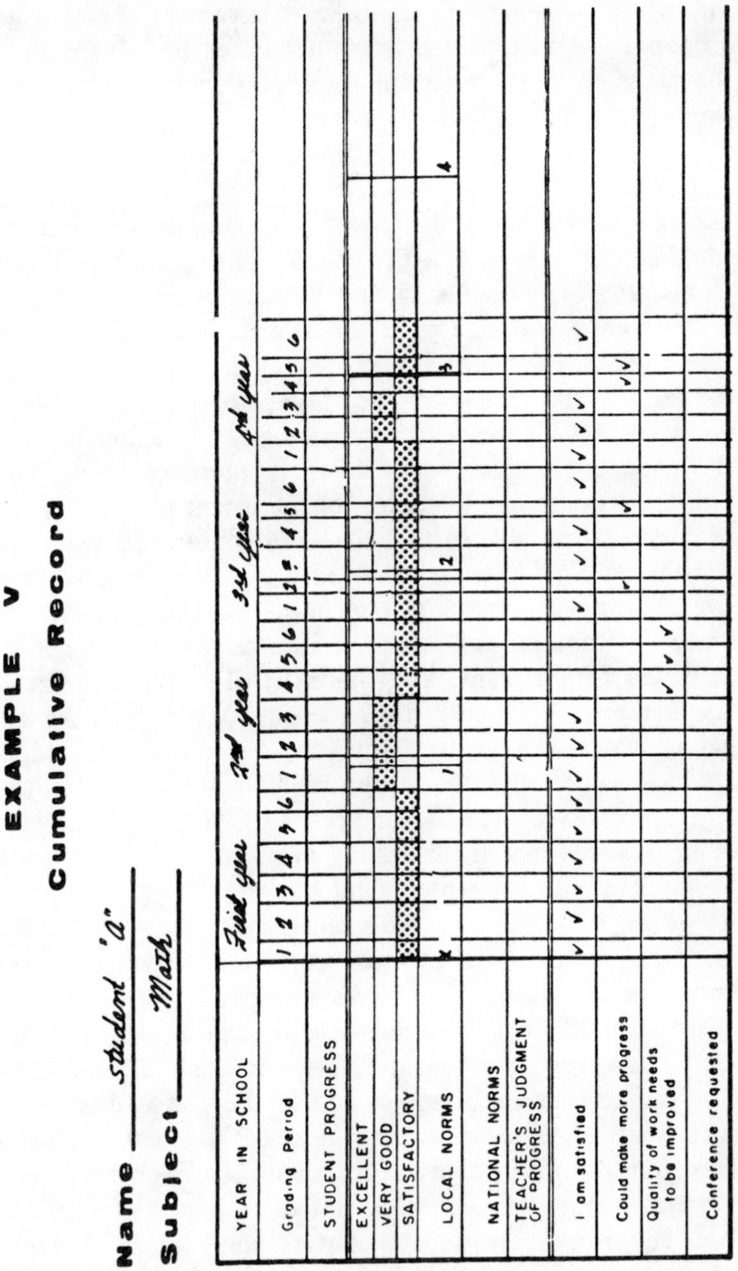

Figure 9-13. *Cumulative record.*

However, it is best that a teacher should try to avoid giving direct advice to a parent. The conference should be ended on a hopeful note of encouragement, reassurance, or restatement of a plan arrived at for cooperative action. If it is deemed necessary, an appointment may be made for further consultation. It is important, throughout this conference, to keep in mind the idea that both teacher and parent are involved in roles that contribute varied essentials to the child's growth.

The parent-teacher-student conference should be preceded by individual conferences held with the child during the year to inform him of his progress. Students should be made aware, well in advance of the conference, which subjects will be discussed at the conference, and those points which are beyond the child's comprehension should be reserved for the parent, in the absence of the child. When the invitation for a conference is issued, a letter of explanation with regard to the content and value of the conference should be sent home to the parent. The keynotes for the parent-teacher conference are, of course, applicable to the three-way conference which should begin with the child present. The teacher may choose to open the conference with a general statement as to the purpose of the three-way conference and then invite the child to express his reactions and future plans. After covering all points with the child, he may then be asked to go outside the classroom so that the teacher and parent may continue the discussion. (From time to time, many parents have indicated their desire that students be allowed to stay for entire conferences.) The second phase of the conference with the parent may then proceed, discussing problems and using "high" to "low" charts to pinpoint achievement.

It is suggested that each teacher maintain some anecdotal records of all conferences to serve as references when conducting future conferences, or writing progress reports.

There should be a convenient and comfortable waiting area provided outside the classroom to be used for the conference, but the door of the conference room should be kept closed at all times during a conference. This waiting area, for the convenience of a parent who might not be able to confer with the teacher immediately upon arrival, should be suitably furnished with a comfortable chair, and a selection of educational literature and magazines. This area should, if possible, be placed at some distance from the conference room, and in any event the door to the latter should be closed, so that conversation cannot be overheard and complete privacy is assured to all concerned.

Advantages and Disadvantages of Conference Method

The obvious advantage of the conference method is the opportunity it provides for the teacher to become more familiar with parents. Among other advantages are:

1. It gives the student an opportunity to answer questions of both parent and teacher about his work.

2. Successful conferences can prove of inestimable value in school-community relations.

The major disadvantage of the conference method stems from the fact that it can be time-consuming. Among other disadvantages are:

1. The difficulty of reaching all parents.

2. The inconvenience such conferences may impose upon parents who are employed.

3. The occasional need to schedule evening as well as regular school day conferences for certain parents.

4. The necessity for cancelling school on those days which are assigned for conferences.

5. The possibility of poorly conducted conferences which may have a detrimental effect on school-community relations.

Periodic Pupil Progress Report

In addition to the above, each time a pupil masters a concept or level of achievement and is ready to progress to another level, a letter or card should be sent home indicating the child's progress. The letter or card should include an outline of the skills, and there should be no delay in forwarding the progress report, as illustrated by Figure 9-14 on page 184.

Advance planning should be undertaken to plan a program for

Dear Parent:

   As you know, your child has been enrolled in a program of
nongraded education. This means that instead of being placed in
a traditional "grade," he will be placed at a particular level in each
subject area. He will then progress from level to level as he absorbs
certain skills within the subject area. So that you will be informed
of your child's progress, periodic reports such as this will be sent
you whenever he progresses from one level to another.

Your child has progressed in _____ from Skill _____
                                            subject area

Level _____, to Skill _____ Level _____.

   If you have any questions with regard to your child's progress
or placement, please feel free to contact me.

                                              Most sincerely,

                                              Principal

Figure 9-14. *Periodic pupil progress report.*

both teachers and parents so that each may be adept at translating
every nuance and meaning of the reporting forms — the teacher to
translate the student's performance accurately, and the parent to
infer the proper information from the reports submitted. Obviously,
this is of the utmost importance if the reporting procedure is to serve
as an efficient instrument to communicate the student's progress.
The astute administrator will also realize that reporting to parents is
an effective way to foster good public relations. Parents seldom tire
of receiving reports on the progress made by their children in school.
   Using the foregoing procedures, a suggested program for
reporting to parents might be as follows:

Method of Reporting to Parents	Sept.	Oct.	Nov.	Jan.	Feb.	Mar.	Apr.	May	June
Parent-Student-Teacher Conference		X					X		
Progress Report Card			X	X				X	X
Parent-Teacher Conference					X			X	

Figure 9-15. *The reporting timetable.*

Suggested Practices When Planning the Nongraded Report Card

The following is a list of recommended practices in planning the nongraded progress report card:

1. There should be no grade designation.
2. Use of terms such as "good," "fair," "excellent," and "poor" should not be used to indicate achievement of any child.
3. Use of scores such as "100," "90," "80," etc. or letters of the alphabet should be avoided.
4. Any methods that make a comparison between the individual child and other children should be avoided.
5. There should be explicit directions on the report cards so that parents can understand the charts and/or graphs if either are used.
6. If possible, during the summer period a team of teachers should plan the report card.
7. A design should be planned only after an attempt has been made to obtain "samples" from other nongraded schools.
8. A program for teachers and parents on learning how to read the report must be planned.
9. The report should be simple enough to provide facile communication to institutions of higher education.
10. The report should indicate the academic progress of the student achieved by dint of his own activities or efforts.
11. There should be clear and concise provisions for indicating the quality of the student's performance.
12. There should be ample provision for entry of teacher judgment of the student's efforts.

13. The report form should not be so complex as to create administrative hardships.

Reporting to parents, regardless of the method used, must serve the purpose of establishing clear intercommunication between the home and the school. It is extremely important that the report be clear, concise and presented in a way so that parents may understand it fully and have no questions in connection with the quantity or quality of the student's progress. When this is accomplished by the school, there is then every opportunity for cooperative parent-teacher-student planning to ensure continued educational growth of each student.

Teacher Training and Reporting Pupil Progress

If a nongraded reporting method is being used to evaluate pupil progress in the program, teachers must be re-educated on how to report a student's progress to parents. If the conference method is being used, an administrator should ask the teacher to become involved in playing the role of both parent and teacher before the actual conference. In addition, there should be an opportunity for the teacher to practice playing the role of the student, the parent and the teacher before a multiple conference takes place. This role playing should portray the "right" way to interact with parents and students, as well as the "wrong" way.

With regard to reporting pupil progress on the reporting form, the administrator should present the teacher with sample reporting forms illustrating progress entries for several representative students with different imaginary rates of progress and performance.

Explaining the Nongraded Report Card to Parents

It is wise for the administrator to call in the parent for a discussion of the pupil progress report card. Some parents have difficulty understanding the chart method of reporting and the graphical representation. The administrator should keep in mind that these reporting forms are contemporary in design and are completely unfamiliar to most parents. Allowance must be made for adjustment, for when parents are unfamiliar with a particular measuring device, they tend to dislike it. Usually, when they have been properly informed as to its interpretation, they agree that it is an improvement over the old method.

SUMMARY

There is no one perfect method of reporting to parents. Each method provides some advantages as well as disadvantages, and each serves a particular purpose. It lies within the purview and discretion of the teacher and the administrator to determine which method, or combination of methods, will prove most successful when considered in conjunction with the calibre of the student population and the character of the adult population of the community.

10. EVALUATING A

NONGRADED PROGRAM

There is no magic in the removal of grade labels. If this is all that takes place, we have the same old school under a new name and a fraud has been perpetrated. There are these administrators who have merely removed the labels and then declared a nongraded school to be in existence.

John I. Goodlad

It is difficult to determine the progress of nongraded programs from research studies. For example, in some studies the authors indicated that there is no difference between the nongraded program and a traditional program. Other studies showed no evidence that students achieve more in a nongraded program than in a traditional program. In yet another study there was indication that students achieve more in a nongraded program in the mathematics area than they do in the reading area. Obviously, a point of immediate concern is the designation of appropriate criteria to identify a particular school as a nongraded school. A recent report by the State Education Department of the University of the State of New York, entitled "The Nongraded School – A Critical Assessment"[1] indicated basically that there was no difference between the nongraded and the traditional school. The author also stated that:

---

[1] William P. McLaughlin, *The Nongraded School – A Critical Assessment*, Associate Director-Research Training Program, The University of the State of New York, The State Education Department, September, 1967.

188

> Since innovations, by definition, are departures from tradition, they replace the old with the new and the innovation must be distinctive. In the research on the nongraded school, this quality is conspicuously absent. One can seldom distinguish the new from the old, the graded from the nongraded, and just what constitutes a nongraded school is anyone's guess.

This attempt to assess nongraded schools demonstrates the need for two areas of concentration: First, the need for establishing guidelines for nongraded education and, second, the need to provide for evaluation of the program once it has been implemented. This book is focused on the need to establish certain nongraded practices. This chapter is based primarily on several methods by which to evaluate and judge these practices once they have been put in motion by the public schools. In this context, the following procedures are suggested as guides for the evaluation of nongraded schools:

Achievement Testing

Achievement tests may be employed if they are used as group surveys to obtain a median level for students at the termination of the traditional program and after a period of implementation of the nongraded techniques. Periodically, each year, the same test should be administered to students in order to determine the extent of progress made. If the school is implementing a nongraded program, there should be the difference evidenced by a rising curve. It is notable that this difference is more apparent among a culturally different student population than in a school in an affluent community.

Most school districts, in attempts to evaluate their nongraded programs, have usually resorted to a system of comparison of reading achievement scores between a controlled group of youngsters from a traditional classroom, and a controlled group of youngsters from a nongraded class. Obviously, if these scores are to be used as the basis for measurement, it should be borne in mind that if a truly nongraded program has been implemented, it will excel over any traditional program in all areas, regardless of the tests or other measuring devices utilized.

Student and Parent Attitude Scale

A committee composed of administrators and teachers should be established to prepare a set of wide-range attitude scales of behavior correlates on the nongraded concept. The set should consist of three parts as described in the Appendix F. Part I is the Student's Evaluation Scale on the Nongraded Program; Part II is the Teacher's Evaluation Scale on the Nongraded Program; Part III is the Parent's Survey regarding Nongraded Education.

Parts I and III of the scales are given to students and parents to determine their reaction to the Nongraded Program. A favorable response would indicate that the administration is well along the way to an effective nongraded program. The attitude scale can also indicate which areas of the educational program need improvement.

A comparison between traditional education and nongraded education is unwarranted because the goal of contemporary education is to individualize and humanize the instructional program. A nongraded program appears to be the most effective method of doing this.

Teacher Attitude Scale

One effective method of evaluating a nongraded program is to request completion by teachers of a Teacher's Evaluation Scale in the Nongraded Concept which reflects their attitudes and feelings about the program.

Part II, the Teacher's Evaluative Scale on the Nongraded Concept, illustrates one sample of an attitude scale designed for teachers. The scale should be administered at least one year after the implementation of the nongraded concept in order to determine the strengths and weaknesses of the program. Therefore, the scale might be administered once every two years to determine whether or not there have been any unfavorable changes in the attitude of the teacher staff with regard to the program. Certainly the teacher attitude should indicate a larger amount of humanization towards children generally and a great deal more sensitivity to the needs of the individual child. This Teacher's Attitude Scale will also indicate teacher reception to the concept of working cooperatively in teams and groups. A chart of the results of the teachers' reactions to the nongraded program, which was administered to 30 teachers, is indicated in Appendix F, Part II.

In general, the evaluative results indicate that the implementation of the nongraded concept has been quite successful. With the exception of items 7 and 11, more than 75 percent of the teachers responded favorably to each item in the Attitudinal Scale, indicating the strength of the program. The area in need of improvement is the Procedure of Reporting to Parents, or Item 11. Apparently, either the report card is too difficult for the parents to comprehend or the Parent-Student-Teacher Conference is too lengthy. This item could very well be the reason for the poor showing in Item 7, indicating that approximately 50 percent of the parents favor the nongraded program, while an approximate 50 percent do not. It would be wise for the administrator to publish the results of the evaluation and distribute them to the teachers for review. The next step would be to contact the parents for a discussion of the procedure for reporting to parents in order to strengthen the weaknesses in this area.

Student Reaction Assessment

One of the more successful ways to determine whether or not a successful nongraded program is being implemented is to have students write an essay on what they believe a nongraded class to be. An immense amount of information may be obtained, as is evidenced by the following samples of such work:

> A nongraded class is a class that has more things to work with than a graded class. It also helps to learn how to work on your own.

> When I was first put in a nongraded class, everything looked so different from the graded class. I like the nongraded, because you have more privileges and things to do such as SRA, Spelling Wheels, tape recorder, and phonograph. I think we also go on more trips, which I enjoy very much.

> I think the nongraded system is fine. I am glad it is started. It gives all students a chance to learn more, and to work at their own rate. The machinery is excellent. The Du Kane is very

good. The tape recorder can also be very useful; the controlled reader which is used by one of the classes, and there are excellent science kits, too.

A nongraded class is a class with children from the grades 3-6. Every child works at his own speed. In order for every child to work at his own speed, we must have many different kinds of materials. You might think that a nongraded class must be confusing, but the way my teacher runs it, it's a lot of fun.

Well, you would have to see it to really understand it. When you first walk in, you might see a group of children with earphones or looking at a film. As you walk around, you may see two children sitting next to each other, doing two different things. One may be doing math and the other science. Then you'd see a rug with children reading stories. As you walk a few more steps, you'd see carrels with the first three people reading quietly, then the last one working on a tape recorder. Right in front are the cubbyholes or boxes. In the boxes are books.

A nongraded class is a class where children learn more than a graded, because if you were in the third grade and you were capable of doing sixth grade work, you would be doing work you already know, so a nongraded class will help you do work you are capable of doing.

In the nongraded classes the children work at their own rate of speed. I think that, up to now, we have done more work than we would really have done in the year in a regular class. To me, the nongraded class is very good.

Nongraded Consultants or Experts

A number of university professors are willing to offer their professional advice towards helping to establish and maintain a nongraded school, for only a nominal fee. It is, of course, imperative for the administrator deciding on a consultant to determine if the person chosen has had successful practical experience with nongraded schools. In addition to reading all of the literature contributed by the consultant, it would also be advisable to visit the schools with which the consultant has been associated to determine if he has really been successful. The reader must remember that if all those who claimed to be, really were, authorities on nongraded education there would be more successful nongraded programs in existence. The fact that there are very few effectively nongraded schools indicates that few self-termed authorities have been really successful in the implementation of nongraded programs.

The following is a list of consultants on the nongraded concept used by Science Research Associates, Inc., at 259 East Erie, Chicago, Illinois, to conduct nongraded workshops:

1. Dr. Robert Anderson, Professor, Graduate School of Education, Harvard University, Cambridge, Massachusetts

2. Dr. Kent Austin, Assistant Superintendent of Instructional Services, Port Washington, Long Island, New York

3. Dr. Walter Baden, Principal, Wheatland-Chili High School, Scottsville, New York

4. Dr. John Bahner, Associate Superintendent of Instruction, Dade County Public Schools, Miami, Florida

5. Dr. Robert Carbone, Special Assistant to the President, the University of Wisconsin, Madison, Wisconsin

6. Mrs. Hope Danielson, Principal, Hamilton Nongraded School, Newton Center, Massachusetts

7. Dr. Martha Dawson, Professor of Education, Hampton Institute, Hampton, Virginia

8. Dr. Joseph Edgington, Superintendent, Reed-Union School District, Belvedere-Tiburon, California

9. Dr. Joe Halliwell, Director of Elementary Education, Cortland State University, Cortland, New York

10. Dr. William Hedges, Director of Curriculum and Research, Clayton Public School, Clayton, Missouri

11. Dr. Maurie Hillson, Professor, Graduate School of Education, Rutgers University, New Brunswick, New Jersey

12. Dr. Elizabeth Z. Howard, Associate Professor of Education, University of Rochester, Rochester, New York

13. Dr. Marshall Jameson, Coordinator of Elementary Schools, Waterford Township, Pontiac, Michigan

14. Mr. Robert Linstone, Principal, Roaring Brook School, Avon, Connecticut

15. Dr. Walter Rehvoldt, Professor of Education, California Western University, San Diego, California

The previously mentioned new world-wide association, Individualizing Instruction and Learning, also provides consulting services. These consulting services are on a contact basis. Specialists in all components of the system for individualizing instruction are available.

The Nongraded Checklist

The administrator can either conduct his own appraisal of the nongraded program, or use the assistance of another administrator in the school district. He may wish to conduct his own appraisal and that of an outsider to determine how closely the two reports are alike. At any rate, the self-appraisal nongraded check list certainly will provide administrators with an opportunity to determine the strong aspects of the nongraded program and the areas needing attention in order to improve the overall educational program. An example of the nongraded check list is as follows:

Administrator's Self-Appraisal Nongraded
Check List

for

_____
date

	Yes	No
1. Terms such as "slow," "average," or "fast" are not used in designating students.		
2. Terms such as "excellent," "good," "fair," or varied alphabetical symbols are abolished from the report card and the grading system.		
3. Ability grouping, homogeneous grouping and tracking are abolished as methods of permanently grouping children.		
4. Homogeneous grouping is used temporarily only to serve the purpose of discovering the needs of individual students.		
5. Skills are not identified by grade levels.		

6. The standard textbook is not the basic instructional tool of the classroom.

7. There are sufficient materials, supplies, textbooks, educational machinery, equipment, and furniture situated in the classroom to afford maximum opportunities for individualization of instruction and flexibility of content.

8. Nongradedness is practiced in all subject areas.

9. Students are not compared to each other or to a national norm.

10. Skill charts or individual study units are available for students.

11. Grade levels are completely removed from all classes.

12. Team teaching is an essential feature of the nongraded program.

13. Teachers were adequately involved in the design and the implementation of the nongraded program.

14. Intelligence Quotient and Academic Achievement scores are not being utilized to group children.

15. The teacher is no longer a disseminator of knowledge, but assumes a variety of roles in order to enable students to learn independently.

16. Parental support has been obtained for the implementation of the nongraded program.

17. Lecturing to students is not the dominant feature of the classroom program.

	Yes	No
18. The Standardized Lesson Plan has been discontinued in the classroom and instead, students are supplied with their own lesson plans, such as individual study units.	___	___
19. The procedure for reporting to parents consists of periodic progress reports, report cards and parent-teacher-student conferences.	___	___

It is essential for administrators to be able to make an effective evaluation of the nongraded program. Not only is this necessary to determine the academic progress of students, but it is also important to gauge the scope of improved performance attributable to use of the nongraded concept so that, where indicated, certain modifications may be made to bring about improvements. To date, the most commonly used method of evaluating the nongraded concept has been to equate scores indicated on academic achievement tests. As an example, in the area of Reading, during the prior program of traditional education, achievement tests were administered and scores recorded. Then, shortly after implementation of the nongraded program, similar achievement tests were administered and the scores from both were compared. Usually the results showed some slight improvement with the use of the nongraded concept, however, the difference could not be called significant. A further unfortunate consequence of using this method of evaluation lies in the failure of these instruments to indicate attitudinal changes on the part of students, teachers, and parents which may have occurred since the implementation of the nongraded concept in the schools. In addition, this method of evaluation makes it impossible to determine the effects of nongraded education on student motivation where independent, individualized study permits a greater amount of self-direction on the part of students.

SUMMARY

Several methods of evaluating the nongraded program
have been illustrated in the foregoing pages. Each method

measures only some certain isolated aspects of the nongraded program. For example, the Students' Evaluation Scale will measure only student attitudes toward the educational process being offered, and will have no relative bearing on the effectiveness of other aspects of the nongraded project. When evaluating the nongraded curriculum, it would perhaps be best to invite experts to come in and render their advice and recommendations. Wherever the administration is interested in equating nongraded education with traditional education, it would be wise to use all of the measuring devices so that no facet of the nongraded program remains unevaluated.

11. CONTEMPORARY EDUCATION

IN CONTEMPORARY TIMES

In two or three years, a student may find himself before a learning instrument panel as dazzling as any astronaut faces in his space capsule. Flick one switch and the logarithm theory is explained in motion, color, and sound. Press another button and a talking book recorded by a leading authority, tells him about the American Revolution. Twist another dial and the computer drills him in irregular verbs......The school of tomorrow will be different not so much because of its new furniture and materials but because of its new ideas.

Ole Sand

We are now living in the midst of an era of extensive and rapid change. Quite often in the hustle of daily existence we passively accept change without really thinking about its enormity in this age as compared with other ages. Was it really less than twenty years ago that atomic scientists discovered how to split the atom, or that a rocket was put into orbit around the earth with the energy from the atom, while there are those among us now making reservations for trips to the moon in the near future? Is it really possible that scientists have created a hydrogen bomb which will obliterate an entire country within minutes? Was it less than three years ago that heart transplants were first attempted on animals, while today there are several human beings who are walking about with the heart of another person functioning in their bodies? Indeed, transplants of various organs such as the kidney, lungs, and eyes have been accomplished with such success that some scientists talk of the eventual ability to replace almost any part of the organism which has stopped functioning with a similar part, much as an automobile is replaced with "spare parts." The most recent possibility in the field of genetics will take all of the guessing out of the birth process when doctors, a few weeks after conception, will be able to indicate whether the newly formed embryo will develop into a male or female fetus. It seems obvious that the older the earth becomes, the more rapidly change occurs because man, in his infinite attempts to manipulate his environment so that he is better served, continues to gain more wisdom each day than at any prior time in history. The change that occurs in all elements of man's life is reflected in the great social changes which are now taking place in American society. Among black Americans; these changes have ranged from a mere existence within the status quo of a semi-caste system, to a plea for integration and, finally, to a demand for separation. Among American students, change is evidenced in demands for a greater voice in affairs which affect their lives, as well as by a studied avoidance in the "hippie" and "yippie" societies of most of those values which their parents held. There seems to be an elusive quality in the air we breathe which serves as a spark for rebellion and change generally. Education cannot escape. As an integral part of the American culture, American public school education must, in the final analysis, affect and be affected by the social and scientific changes which are taking place. Unfortunately, for too long a time, education has lagged behind and hopefully, in the very near future, it will take great strides to catch up to and remain abreast of the times.

Many of the problems which we are encountering in the public schools which serve a predominant number of culturally different students arise from the negative elements contained in a traditional education program. Traditional education has done so much to thwart the intellectual growth of these students that many administrators are continually frustrated in their attempts to provide them with an adequate education. The only direction left in which to move must be toward a change in the present traditional structure so that the diverse, individual needs of these students can be met by the public schools. A major problem confronting educators is their own long indoctrination in the precepts of traditional education, which tends to deter them from the drastic changes necessary to improve the educational system.

Preparing Today for Tomorrow's Changes

All who are involved in the educational program today must give way to change, even as men and women working in many various fields must accommodate to change. Parents, students, administrators, teachers, school and university officials must all move forward in preparation for tomorrow's educational changes.

1. The Role of Parents — Parents must be receptive to change and must be willing to make an active effort to arouse a rebirth of that faith they once had in the efficacy of public school education. This can only be accomplished by an obvious change in attitudes, methods, and goals on the part of professionals who man the public schools. Where current conditions are not satisfactory or become unsatisfactory, parents must be willing to take the initiative in constructive approaches to bring about change. They must give more time to becoming personally involved in educational organization and procedures, demanding and taking advantage of opportunities to become familiar with successful innovative methods of learning, and visiting schools where these techniques are being utilized. They must demand a voice and a role in decision-making policies of the public school system so that they can appreciate the operational intricacies of bringing about change and the conditions which occur as a result. In particular, parents must be ready and willing to accept the added expenses and increased costs which constructive changes generate. One source of irrevocable increased costs lies in the area of professional salaries. In addition, experimental research must be conducted to determine the feasibility of particular ideas for constructive change in order to determine their true merit as public school goals. Major responsibilities fall upon parents in their new role in public school education, but this is as it should be. However, their new role as guardians, investigators and initiators can only be effective if they constantly think in futuristic terms of what should be and what will be, rather than rely on what was good enough for them and on past educational practices. Economic, social, and political conditions now demand and will continue to demand a different kind of national educational policy than has ever been adhered to in any past era of American history.

2. *The Role of Educational Professionals* – Educational professionals must provide the impetus for viable ways to end traditional instruction which has proven ineffective. They must pave the way for and be highly receptive to constructive change, because until and unless these changes come our entire nation will be detrimentally affected. Educators have a great deal to ponder over in terms of meeting their ever-increasing responsibilities for preparing themselves to promote change and support actively those elements which promise to bring success to their endeavors to teach. The intellectual responsibility is tremendous in terms of keeping intimately abreast of current developments, educational research, and new techniques and methods. A professional in education has much the same responsibility as a professional in medicine to take advantage of new methods and technology for diagnoses, as well as of new prescriptions for cure and remediation, to be followed by well-founded prognoses for the emergence of a healthy and well-rounded intellect. Educational professionals must not be afraid to venture into unexplored areas, and attempt new methods, always bearing in mind that research and experimentation are the only means by which education can progress. They must not be afraid to experiment with new methods and ideas to improve a given condition or situation in learning. Where would the country be today if great men like Plato, Socrates, Dewey and George Washington Carver had not pioneered with what they considered the best techniques for imparting information to others. What will be, perhaps, most difficult, is the necessity for educators to assign priorities to their life goals. By this is meant the dire necessity for educators to determine whether their primary goal is to "make money" or "make minds." Each goal has its own sacrifices and its own rewards, and it is essential that potential educators or working professionals recognize that it is only in very rare instances that both goals are reached in the field of education. In this context, educational professionals must be willing to de-emphasize monetary rewards in favor of a concentration on those rewards intrinsic to the educational profession: providing intellectual leadership, stimulating

new thought, and moulding the minds of other men who will lead future civilizations. In this way, educators, perhaps more than any other professional, capture the secret of immortality. Educational professionals must take the lead in establishing research committees which are active in seeking and trying new developments and alternative ways of performing certain acts conducive to learning. Industry, for instance, has made its great technological advances because of its massive regular expenditure of thousands of dollars for research. In contrast, education has only recently begun to initiate large-scale activity in this area. Unfortunately, educators tend to continue doing what they have been doing in the past, even though they can see the unsuccessful results of these procedures. Much of this, of course, is a direct result of a dearth of educational research which might provide alternatives to what has proven unsuccessful. Educators should expend every effort to visit innovative schools throughout the country, discuss the results of these innovations and then, if they seem practicable, bring these innovations back to their own school districts. All educators must put forth a concentrated and continuing effort to uproot the problems existing in most traditional classrooms, either by taking advantage of opportunities for additional preparation and training, or by taking sabbatical leaves to gain professional experiences through extensive travel and study which will re-orient them to changes taking place in education. Educational administrators and professional educators' associations must not hesitate to pluck out ineffectual teachers and to encourage those teachers with open minds and new ideas who will be dedicated to the task of bringing about constructive changes in education, motivated not by personal opportunism. but by humanitarian urges. Educators must be willing to accept the fact that social changes now demand that parents and students take on more active roles in education, if constructive measures are to bring about improvements in education.

3. *The Role of Institutions of Higher Education* – One of the largest obstacles to change in education is the cautious and traditional attitude of our colleges and universities, many of which are staffed with diehard professors who, instead of being the leaders of change, prefer to retain the comfortable status quo. These professors who find it impossible to accept curriculum change must move or be moved aside to make room for those who are willing to risk everything to gain the maximum goal of turning out the most

effective educators to be found anywhere in the world. America has assumed a leading role internationally in many areas but it remains a sad commentary that education is not recognized as one of these areas. Throughout the course of history, man has made numerous changes — some bad, some good — to improve the health, education and welfare of his fellow man. While America has made great technological advances, the educational lag still remains high. Universities must assume a leading role; they must experiment on much the same large scale as our inventors have; and they must change their theories and practices to bring about constructive change. Universities must begin to offer courses such as "Changing Traditions in Education," "Contemporary Education," "Nongraded Education" and "Team Teaching." A glance at almost any college bulletin will see an absence of courses such as those listed above. Some states have changed their specific course requirements to general course requirements for teacher certificates. For example, in New York it will no longer be necessary for teacher candidates to take specified courses, such as history of education, psychology, art, etc. to obtain certification. Instead, they will only be required to complete a specified number of hours in certain general areas in order to acquire certification. Although the State Education Department has taken this drastic step, most institutions of higher education have failed to take the lead in revamping their curriculum to include more contemporary courses. Unfortunately, American universities and colleges have consistently failed to exhibit the leadership they should in order to spearhead change. As a result, students at colleges and universities are in turmoil, and unless these institutions prepare now for changes, the so-called "social revolution" will continue for years to come.

　　4. The Role of Students — Students will be the major recipients of the benefits of change, and they too must undertake the personal task of preparing themselves mentally to accept the changes in education offered them. They must internalize an attitude which will permit them to become more involved in their educational destiny. Because they are to be on the receiving end of educational programs designed to meet their needs, it is essential that they have a voice, an opinion, and a sense of complete participation. The students themselves must take the lead in requesting curriculum changes which imbue their studies with more relevance to the life-realities. Students must be willing to embrace a positive approach to educational change and be willing also to exercise a measure of self-restraint in their demands for unrealistic or non-constructive changes in terms of primary educational goals.

5. *The Role of State Education Officials* – State Education officials who have formerly occupied remote thrones in the educational hierarchy must also step down to meet change, both in their own structure and goals and in their interrelationships with their school districts. They must not continue to feel that they have the irrevocable answers to which no alternative solutions may prove better. They must no longer make authoritarian recommendations which must be followed simply because, in the opinion of the State Education Department, these recommendations are the ones which will produce the desired results. State education departments must be willing to accept, and indeed should be the forerunners in, research and experimentation projects to set the pattern for change. They must assume an increasingly close association with school districts to help them bring about constructive changes and, where constructive change has occurred in one school district, assume the responsibility for seeing that all other school districts have an opportunity to incorporate certain features of the improvement, or adopt it in its entirety. A major burden which state education departments will be called upon to accept is the necessarily added expense incurred in subsidizing certain experimental projects which school districts wish to implement. They must allow increasing availability of their research departments and experts, to work in close coordination with those school districts undertaking experimentation and to remain involved throughout the evaluative process for the program.

Future Developments

Education cannot afford to lag behind any longer, and must experience a complete revitalization if it is to meet the needs of the young individuals who will constitute the 60 to 70 million American youngsters requiring a more than just adequate public school education in the future. Education must absorb and reflect the contemporary world and contemporary needs of all students, and in anticipation of their future needs must provide them with the humanism, the sensitivity, and the intellectual excellence which changing concepts, educational technology and instruction for the individual can provide.

Predicting Education Changes

It is to be expected that the following predictions for educational change will become the sudden realities of tomorrow's schools.

1. Education will be nurtured in an extremely humane environment, meeting the needs of individual students with the nongraded concept which will serve as the foundation on which schools are to be built.

2. As a general rule, students will be admitted to school much earlier than in past years and, in line with this, it will be commonplace for a pregnant mother to receive special training dealing with her relationship with her child during the period immediately following delivery through the pre-school years.

3. Education will become doubly effective with the aid of new scientific discoveries which enable controls to be exercised over the mentality of youngsters. Genetic engineering has already had astounding success in the removal of animal embryos to determine sex and the replacement of the embryo for the completion of the foetal phase, so it is not too far-fetched to expect that determination of mental retardation and physiological disturbances may also be made at this very early stage. Then early treatment may be administered so that few children will actually be born with mental deficiencies arising out of physiological causes.

4. In the field of education today, millions and millions of dollars are being wasted annually because of our persistence in closing down school physical plants for approximately 50 percent of the year. There is no corporate enterprise in existence which would contemplate such foolhardy expense as allowing a well-equipped structure to stand in idleness for a half year without producing. In the future, more and more school districts will begin to utilize their expensive plants for as much of the year as becomes possible with extended school year designs. Even at present, more than 50 foreign countries have begun to utilize their school facilities for as many as 230 school days in extended school year designs, and there is no doubt that the increasing cost of operating schools will make this practice more widespread.

5. We are now beginning to see the spread of educational technology which will continue more and more rapidly to assume a major role in assisting teachers in drill remedial work, compensatory education, and individualized instruction. Concomitant with the

increased emphasis on the use of educational technology and teaching machines, a necessarily greater emphasis will be placed on instilling humanism as an integral part of the educational system.

6. There will be world-wide acceptance of computerized education as a tool of maximum efficiency which can provide extended dimensions in the instructional program. Not only will computer use be extensively utilized to encompass various facets of the entire secondary school program, but their use will also be increased in elementary schools. Students' research time will be greatly diminished, enabling them to receive more information in a shorter period of time, and computer use will also enable them to obtain knowledge when it is most useful – almost at the instant they seek it.

7. Educational television will be a major tool of education, and its value in the education of culturally different youngsters will be widely acknowledged. More schools will automatically provide programs in which the culturally different child will operate the equipment as well as plan and produce his own "live" segments, which will then be circulated widely. The culturally different child will be enabled to improve his self-image; his particular needs will be more widely recognized and accepted; and all the "other worlds" will be brought that much closer so that the unknown will no longer be a subject of fear or revulsion. Today we have only an inkling of the many possible uses of educational television in the educational process. Educational television will, of course, do much to bring humanism into the school plant.

8. With the increased emphasis on humanism in education, teachers, students, and community members will be provided with sensitivity training in schools where group therapy will be conducted by a leader trained in the psychology of day-to-day, experience-oriented sessions. Comfortable living room lounges where sensitivity training sessions can be conducted will become commonplace in the school plant. Sensitivity training will occupy an important place at all levels of the educational establishment as man increasingly becomes aware of the dire necessity of learning to live in harmony with his fellow man if neither is to be annihilated.

9. The physical plants which house our schools will revert to plans very similar to the old one-room schoolhouse design, except that they will be so enlarged that they will be able to accommodate

several hundred students at one time. The interiors will be large and spacious with very few visible walls. The ultimate in flexibility and efficiency will be achieved by:

    a. Installation of wall-to-wall carpeting on all floors to provide an atmosphere of warmth and comfort while, at the same time, minimizing sound distractions.

    b. Utilization of furniture and equipment that is highly flexible in use and not fixed in permanent settings.

    c. Numerous collapsible partitions which can be used to provide adequate grouping procedures easily.

10. Students will have a greater voice in their education, all the way from the elementary level right through to the secondary level and institutions of higher learning.

Most of the present required rules for student behavior within the school milieu will be greatly modified. Students will learn in a much more relaxed atmosphere where it is possible that smoking, eating or sleeping in class will not be strictly verboten. What is to be envisioned is a school that meets the individual needs of each student as they occur, so that if a student has missed breakfast and is hungry before the lunch period, it will no longer be criminal for him to eat in class; or if a student is addicted to smoking in order to lower anxieties, then he will be allowed to smoke in class; and if a student who finds it necessary to work outside of school hours is overcome with fatigue during class, he will not be penalized if he drops his head on his desk for a short period.

11. Many more schools will begin to make effective use of learning laboratories by taking their students to the Museum of Natural History, to the Museum of Art, to the Hayden Planetarium; to newspapers and publishing houses to study journalism and creative writing; and to tne public library for social studies and other subject areas. Learning will not be confined to the classroom, and these natural laboratories will regularly accommodate large and small groups of students.

12. Because of early childhood and continuous progress programs, many students will be entering and leaving school at earlier ages. It is possible to predict that many students will be graduating from secondary schools at 14 or 15, and from college at 18 or 19.

13. In higher education, the undergraduate program may be replaced by a five-year program which awards the masters degree

and, concurrently with the achievements which continuous progress and nongraded education permit, it is entirely possible that some students will complete this program in less than five years.

14. Students will be required to determine at an earlier age, perhaps in the middle school, the area in which they are most interested in concentrating their studies. In this way, a student can complete many of his basic courses in his major area while still in secondary school and take advanced work immediately upon entrance to college. This, in turn, will give more students an opportunity to get practical experience in their field as, for example, interns, assistant teachers, associate social workers, associates in law, etc., before accepting positions immediately upon graduation from college in which they are now designated as academicians with no practical experience.

15. In order to provide an educational program which is relevant to the realities of each of its students, school districts of the future will no doubt have students and teachers create and publish their own textbooks and materials which are reflective of the interests of the sub-society living in that particular school district. This will be done primarily in an effort to improve the self-image of these students and inspire in them a sense of their own dignity and worth, regardless of their backgrounds. These efforts which have improvement of the self-image as their goal can do much to motivate achievement in academic and non-academic subjects.

Constructive educational changes will come. They must come because of the many revolutions occurring, not only in this country, but in the entire world, where young people are demanding that leaders of today change the old traditions to more viable procedures which meet the needs of modern students. The younger generation, quite rightly, realizes that it cannot survive in a contemporary society by adhering to the customs of its foreparents. Young people are asking for change and they will continue to insist that change be made to satisfy their individual needs.

Appendix A

A Bulletin on the Nongraded Concept

NONGRADED BULLETIN

January, 1968   *Issue I   Milton Olive Elementary School*

Implications of the Nongraded Concept

Within a few weeks, our school will arrive at the end of its first nongraded semester. We think it highly appropriate at this time to look back and undertake an evaluation of the program to see what has been accomplished and what still needs to be accomplished. In order to do this, we believe an examination of our school to see how it measures up to the three basic principles inherent in the nongraded concept will prove to be enlightening.

The Nongraded Attitudes

In the organization and maintenance of a nongraded school, it is important that educators always bear in mind the variations in learning ability which exist among all students. At the same time, educators must proceed on the premise that variations in academic ability are no less commonplace than physiological and temperamental variations. Indeed, there will be individual differences in:

- Bodily structure
- Behavioral and emotional tendencies
- Bodily pigmentation
- Cultural orientation
- Interest direction and learning potential

These individual differences must strongly influence choice of curriculum; variety and content of instructional materials and techniques; and the pace at which instruction is to proceed.

Implications of the Nongraded Concept for the Student

Educators who are sensitively aware of individual differences among children are important agents in each child's development – physically, mentally and emotionally. The elements of the nongraded concept which permit each child to grow and to learn according to his potential, unhampered by restrictions to progress imposed in the traditional graded system and unexposed to the personal disparagement of failing grades, play an important part in the child's attempts to grow, to acquire confidence and to develop a good self-image. Specifically, the composition of the nongraded program which inures to each pupil's benefit should include all of the following elements:

1. Students are provided, within the school setting, with opportunities for interaction with other children, both similar and dissimilar in terms of interests, ability, potential and personality.

2. Students may increase their rate of progress in strong areas of special skills, interests and ability.

3. There is enough flexibility within the program to allow students to profit, in terms of concentrating on weak areas and skill acquisition, by increased expenditures of time spent in individual instruction, independent study, and large, medium or small group instruction, as indicated.

4. More instructors with special skills, talents and abilities are available to each student.

5. Each student is an entity unto himself and is judged not by other students, but by the results of his own endeavors measured against his own abilities, interests and potential.

If you have been occasionally perplexed during the past year, do not feel uneasy. We are aware of the highly complex nature of the nongraded philosophy which represents one of the most challenging educational innovations to have occurred in many centuries. However, each child is a wonderful and complex creation, and the educational process cannot be simple under such circumstances, especially in view of the highly complex world in which man lives today. The nongraded concept, if thoughtfully and appropriately implemented, heralds the birth of a new public school system with a plethora of possibilities for educators to provide high quality education for both the "advantaged" and the "disadvantaged" children who will be the citizens of America — Twenty-First Century.

Enrichment Opportunities in the Nongraded School

The flexibility of the nongraded school when compared with the rigidity of the traditional graded system affords the educator copious opportunities to incorporate enriching experiences into all levels of the school program. For example, flexible scheduling provides for the time differential necessary to allow exploration of ideas and suppositions over and above the "minimum requirement." This is especially important in areas where a student demonstrates an especial ability and interest. To a large degree, the teacher's creativity ceases to remain stifled as the challenge of open-ended units and projects is presented. Additionally, resources of home, school and community may be integrated through the medium of individual and group cooperative endeavors and experiences.

Appendix B

A Circular
Requesting Parents to Support
the Principal's Nongraded Plan

PARENTS

SUPPORT THE PRINCIPAL'S NONGRADED PLAN

COME OUT

TO THE NEXT

BOARD OF EDUCATION MEETING

TUESDAY NIGHT

MARCH 7, 1967

8:00 P.M.

STRAIGHT PATH SCHOOL

DO YOU BELIEVE that schools should develop a plan whereby each student can move through the educational program on the basis of his individual learning ability and achievements?

DO YOU BELIEVE that it is important for schools to provide instruction which emphasizes the needs and interests of each child?

DO YOU BELIEVE that the intellectual development of a student can best be provided through an instructional program which gives each student opportunities for decision-making and scientific problem solving, and which provides the background necessary for intelligent use of knowledge?

IF YOU BELIEVE these points, then . . . *you believe*

IN THE NONGRADED CONCEPT

However, believing is not enough!!!

THE PRINCIPAL NEEDS YOUR SUPPORT!!!

Demonstrate to the Board that you support his program on the Nongraded Concept by your attendance at the next Board meeting.

LET US ALL JOIN HANDS TOGETHER TO BRING TO WYANDANCH THE FINEST EDUCATION ON LONG ISLAND

Appendix C

A Handbook
on the Nongraded Concept
for Parents

A Report to Parents

· *For*

· *Improved*

· *Education*

JAMES LEWIS, JR.
District Principal

MESSAGE TO PARENTS

This letter and the enclosures in it are intended as a report to you about certain necessary changes which are to be made in the organizational structure of the present educational program. These changes are being made for the most important reason for which change should ever be made in a school — to better the education we are offering to your children so that their progress may be determined by their individual learning capacity and their particular interest levels. Since, in whatever we attempt, even in education, there are always human imperfections to be allowed for, we do not consider this change to be an "instant" panacea which will correct all of the dissatisfaction you may have with regard to education within the school district and, perhaps, generally. However, we concur in the opinion of many other educators that this change which involves the initiation of a new concept - the Nongraded School - will serve to imbue our students with a healthier, more wholesome attitude toward school while, at the same time, permitting the school to better fulfill its obligations to each student.

In order to provide each child with the opportunity for continuous progress in school, the nongraded school utilizes achievement levels as a measurement of ability and skills attained as a substitute for grade levels. In other words, there are no grade designations and each child, dependent upon the skills he possesses, is placed either on the primary or on the intermediate level.

Throughout the nation, the nongraded program of education is being implemented and gaining widespread and rapid acceptance. At present, it can be roughly estimated that more than 30 percent of the nation's schools have adopted many of the features of nongraded education, and it is reasonable to predict that the nongraded philosophy will achieve worldwide acceptance and serve as the foundation for the school of the future.

I have made recommendations to the board of education for the implementation of the nongraded program in this district beginning in September 1967 — initially, at the elementary level and, eventually, on the secondary level. Careful planning and coordination is being undertaken so that at each step in the nongraded school the teacher will be fully aware of the individual growth pattern and educational needs of each of her pupils. I am sure you are aware, even as we are, that progression in school work can only occur when the child is physically, emotionally and mentally developed to fully absorb such work or curriculum. In consideration of this, the nongraded curriculum has been adapted to the child, as opposed to the old, traditional method of adapting the child to the curriculum. This program sets as its goal the provision of maximum achievement for each child in the school district, at his own level of ability and rate of progress and within the range of his interest levels.

I would also like to take this opportunity to appeal to you for your continued cooperation with the school and its teachers so that all of us together may serve as a single, unified agent intent upon fostering better education for the students in this school district.

Principal

*   *   *   *   *   *

CHILDREN ARE DIFFERENT

** Some are tall; some are short

** Some are overly shy; some are aggressive

** Some are weak; some are strong

** Some get their teeth early; some late
** Some are thin; some are fat
** Some are skillful; some uncoordinated
** Boys generally develop physically more
   slowly than girls
** Some walk early; some late

*   *   *   *   *   *

THEREFORE, ISN'T IT REASONABLE TO BELIEVE THAT . . .

** Children are not ready to read at the same chronological age.
** Children should have the opportunity to learn and to progress at
   their own rate.
** Children's interests vary.
** Children progress through their education at different rates of
   speed.
** Children should progress continuously without needlessly
   omitting or repeating any part of the curriculum.

** Children should not be expected to learn that which is beyond their capacities.

** No child should have to wait for slower or less mature children.

** Children do not gain confidence by repeated experiences of failure.

** Children should be permitted to develop at their own rate of learning.

** A feeling of success during the early stages of education gives children a wholesome attitude toward their entire school life.

*   *   *   *   *   *

NOW LET'S EXAMINE THE PRESENT-DAY GRADED SCHOOL TO DETERMINE SOME OF ITS FAULTS

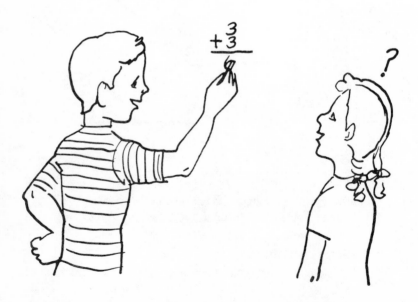

** Children of the same chronological age are expected to develop to the same extent in one year.

** Children not measuring up to adult standards of measured accomplishment in a school year are labeled failures.

** Failure necessitates repetition of grade and curriculum.

** Failing fosters poor self-concept.

** Movement through grades (curricular) is based upon yearly promotion. If a child is retained or accelerated, he would repeat or miss a complete school year.

** There are fixed standards of achievement within a set time, creating pressures on the child and the teacher.

** The gifted child is held back and the slower child is left behind.

** Students who fail are labeled underachievers, poor readers, or slow learners.

** Teacher teaches the group of extremely varied abilities and achievement levels as though all children are the same.

*   *   *   *   *   *

WHAT ARE SOME OF THE ADVANTAGES
OF THE NONGRADED SCHOOL PLAN?

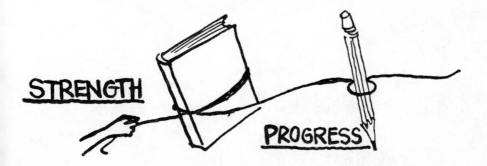

** Children learn to listen to each other and to respect what each one has to say regardless of age, size, or sex. Individual differences are recognized and accepted.

** No child is a failure; instead continuous progress is made at a slower pace.

** The child progresses through the education program as rapidly or as slowly as he can manage the curriculum. Most pupils would take three years to complete the program; however, some pupils may need only two years, and others may require four years.

** Children never experience the frustration which comes from a report of failure.

** Students enjoy school because they are achieving.

** The program promotes good work habits by helping children do challenging tasks within the range of their individual abilities.

** The feeling of success a child experiences in the school program gives him a more wholesome attitude toward his school as a whole.

** It develops keener powers of observation and identification of instructional needs on the part of the teacher.

** It eliminates the stigma which may accompany non-promotion at the end of the school year.

** Nongraded plan takes pressure off children and results in fewer emotional problems and less trouble with pupil behavior.

** The classroom teacher uses a variety of education materials, such as several textbooks, supplementary books, programmed materials and education machines to individualize the instructional program, thereby meeting the individual needs of each child.

*   *   *   *   *   *

SOME QUESTIONS AND ANSWERS FOR PARENTS ON THE NONGRADED CONCEPT . . .

Q. What is a nongraded elementary school?
A. It is the organization of the elementary school which provides for individual differences and allows children to progress at their

own rate according to their needs and abilities. It also allows children to learn in an orderly, continuous way. The curriculum is organized and based upon skill sequences or steps replacing the traditional organization of grades one through six. The curricula subjects are adopted to the child's ability to learn the necessary skills or steps involved.

Q. What is the essential difference between the concept "grade" and the concept "level"?

A. The term "grade" means that a child must complete certain items of achievement within a time limit, or he fails. The term "level" means that a child is permitted to complete certain items of achievement according to his ability to achieve without a time limit. A child never fails in a nongraded school.

Q. How is the child placed at the proper level?

A. The Botel Reading Inventory is given to all children to determine on which reading level the child should be placed. Teacher evaluation, reading tests, mathematics tests, and standardized achievement tests also serve as guides in proper placement.

Q. How long will a child be expected to remain with the same teacher?

A. There is no set rule. Placement is flexible depending upon the child's individual needs and teacher. Often a child will stay with the same teacher for two years. This gives the child and the teacher ample opportunity to know each other.

Q. When does a child go from one level to another?

A. When he has mastered the skills and materials of one level, the child progresses to the next succeeding level.

Q. How do parents know which level their child is on?

A. A written notice is sent to the parent.

Q. When does a child leave the elementary school?

A. Intermediate students usually enter the junior high school after three years. Some pupils may require more or less time.

Q. How will parents know how their child is doing?

A. Carefully recorded data will be kept regarding the progress of each child. Through regularly scheduled and arranged parent-teacher conferences and progress reports, the parents will be informed of the progress of their child. Marking is done according to the individual child and not by a local or national norm.

Appendix D

A Nongraded Workshop Program

WYANDANCH SCHOOLS

PROFESSIONAL CONFERENCE DAY

April 10th, 1968

MILTON L. OLIVE SCHOOL, WYANDANCH, N.Y.

9:00 – 9:30   *Coffee and Cake*

9:30 – 10:30   *Dr. Charles Raebeck*
Director of Teacher Education
Adelphi Suffolk College
"Analysis of Contemporary
Revolution in Education"

10:30 – 10:40   *Mr. James Lewis, Jr.*
District Principal

10:40 – 12:00   *Nongraded Workshops – as scheduled*
Mr. John Adams
Workshop Advisor
Adelphi Suffolk College

12:00 – 1:00   *LUNCH*

1:00 – 2:30   *Presentation of Nongraded Workshop*
Reports

NONGRADED WORKSHOPS

I.   SUBJECT: Placement and Grouping   *Room 1*

Questions to report on:

    1. What is the best grouping arrangement for the
nongraded classes?

Teacher Assignment:

II.   SUBJECT: Orientation for Parents and Reporting   *Room 2*
to Parents

Questions to report on:

    1. What steps should be taken to orient parents
for nongraded program?
    2. How is pupil progress best reported?

Teacher Assignment:

III. SUBJECT: Materials and Equipment Needed for   *Room 3*
Implementation of a Nongraded
Concept

Questions to report on:

    1. What materials are needed?
    2. How do we best supply materials for
nongraded program?
    3. What equipment is recommended for
nongraded program?
    4. What are the place of the needs for
curriculum guides in a nongraded program?

Teacher Assignment:

IV.   SUBJECT: Continuous Evaluation of the   *Room 4*
Nongraded Program

Questions to report on:

    1. What criteria do we use to determine the
success of a nongraded program?

Teacher Assignment:

V.   SUBJECT: Diagnostic Testing – Pre and Post   *Room 5*

Questions to report on:

    1. Should commercial or district-made tests be
used?
    2. How should test results be used?

Teacher Assignment:

VI. SUBJECT: Individually Prescribed Instruction and   *Room 6*
                 Its Implications to the Nongraded
                 Program

Questions to report on:

    1. How is socialization provided for?
    2. What are the advantages of IPI?
    3. What is the connection between IPI and
       nongraded education?

Teacher Assignment:

VII. SUBJECT: Use of Teacher Aides   *Room 7*

Questions to report on:

    1. What training and what qualifications are
       needed?
    2. How are teacher aides best used?

Teacher Assignment:

VIII. SUBJECT: Preparing Teachers for the Nongraded   *Room 8*
                 Program

Questions to report on:

    1. What more must be done for implementation
       of a nongraded program?

Teacher Assignment:

Appendix E

A Preliminary
Nongraded Implementation Plan

PRELIMINARY NONGRADED IMPLEMENTATION PLAN

Introduction

Beginning in the September, 1968 school year, there will be complete implementation of the nongraded concept in the elementary schools of Wyandanch School District. Educational research has supported the contention of knowledgeable educators that the traditional method of homogeneously grouping children of varying abilities and interests, yet expecting all to complete a rigidly prescribed mass of material for their particular grade level, has not accomplished the goal of offering equal educational opportunity to all students. In a particular grade, there will be many children with different personalities, different interests, different abilities, and different rates of achievement. However, the traditional program, which demands completion by all students of the grade material, presumes that all are equally capable of absorbing and retaining this material and ignores the aptitudes of the individual.

Several partial attempts have been made to supplement the more obvious weaknesses in a traditionally oriented school system by using the tools of compensatory education, remedial designs in reading, ability grouping, and other subtle, well-meaning, but ineffective attempts to erase the ills wrought by an antiquated system of public education. As a matter of fact, the most obvious results of these attempts seem to lie in the area of a whole new field of esoteric semantics such as "culturally deprived," "slow learners," "disruptive child," "educable problem children," and a whole gamut of similar terms which might fill a "handy reference book." It is entirely reasonable, under the circumstances and with the vast array of research material which is available decrying the inefficiency of the traditional methods, to seek a complete transformation of educational methods — transformation which is built on a humanization of the educational program so that the needs of the individual student are given primary importance. The nongraded philosophy seems to be the ideal vehicle for such transformation.

Therefore, we shall endeavor to reorganize the elementary educational program and make the humanistic transformation of education in Wyandanch a reality. This humanization will be accomplished by building the educational program around the interests and values of the individual student, seeking new ways and means to meet the needs of the individual child, rather than attempting to fit all students into a preconceived program.

Projected Elements of the Overall Nongraded Program

The nongraded program will consist of five phases in the 12-year educational program:

1. *Pre-Primary Phase:*

This phase will be divided into an Informal and a Formal Phase. The former begins in the home with the instruction of children of 18 months of age and continues until approximately age three, at which time the child enters the Formal Stage and receives concrete educational experience in attendance at the Martin Luther King Jr., School.

Prior to beginning school, the individual child will receive a battery of tests designed to determine his level of maturation, perception, sensory development, and overall readiness to learn. Depending on the results of these tests, the child will be placed on a level designated by alphabets. Here, the first problem will be to determine what kind of tests, and, if necessary, devise new readiness tests to be administered to children in the Early Childhood Program and the first grade. Age is not to be considered when placing these children. For example, the child may be six years old, but functioning on Level G. Level G would be used to identify the child who has sensory and perceptual difficulty combined with defective speech patterns. In Level G, he will receive specialized education, training, and guidance to cure these difficulties and bring him up to his maximum achievement level of functioning in these areas. When the maximum level is achieved in this phase, the child is ready for the basic elementary nongraded program of education to which he is accordingly admitted.

2. *Primary Phase:*

The Primary Phase will cover the first, second, and third grades. The first year students will be heterogeneously grouped for instruction. The second and third year students will be multi-aged, and heterogeneously grouped. In the Primary Phase of the educational program, the child is required to master all of the levels before going on to the Intermediate Phase. The Primary Phase will take place both at the Martin Luther King Jr., School and at the Straight Path School. Explanation will be given to parents about these procedures for grouping students in the initial phases of their education.

3. *Intermediate Phase:*

The Intermediate Phase will encompass the traditional grades four through six and will be housed at the Milton Olive School.

4. *Junior Phase:*

The Junior Phase will encompass the traditional junior high school and will be housed at the Wyandanch Memorial Junior-Senior High School.

5. *Senior Phase:*

The Senior Phase will encompass the traditional senior high school grades and will be housed at the Wyandanch Memorial Junior-Senior High School.

All of the foregoing phases will overlap, as may be seen from the following diagram, and there will be no clearcut delineation between one phase and the next.

Pre-Primary Phase

    Primary Phase

        Intermediate Phase

            Junior Phase

                Senior   Phase

Basic Composition of the Nongraded Program

Humanism, a basic ingredient of this program, will be effectuated generally by application of the nongraded concept in the following methods:

1. Team teaching.
2. Effective utilization of teacher aides, intern teachers, and student aides.
3. Utilization of individually prescribed instruction in mathematics.
4. Implementation of individual study units in various other subject areas, such as reading, language arts, and social studies.

5. Utilization of science laboratories to foster individualization of instruction.

6. Team learning — creating a situation where children are arranged in groups according to common interests, within which groups, teaching and learning from each other may occur.

7. Multi-age grouping — for the purpose of preventing any regression to traditionalism.

Tentatively, all the materials for the individually prescribed instruction in mathematics should be in the school district by the middle of June. In order to facilitate teacher training, we are contemplating delaying student attendance by approximately one week in September, so that teachers may receive uninterrupted training during that time.

Teaching arrangements for the 1968-69 school year will involve the formation of teams of teachers, who will be identified by letters of the Greek alphabet; i.e., Alpha Team, Beta Team, Gamma Team, Delta Team and Epsilon Team. Each team shall consist of three or four teachers, teacher aides, an intern teacher and student aides. It is important to keep in mind one of the most basic precepts of the nongraded concept — that the teacher's role is no longer that of a lecturer or verbal disseminator of information. The new teacher role is that of activator, stimulator, advisor or catalyst, if you will, depending on the needs of the individual student. The teacher's role is flexible and ever-changing and includes the responsibility of determining the specific needs of individual students and planning individualized activities to meet these needs. This obviously necessitates great familiarity on the part of the teacher with lesson material over a wide range of topics at an equally wide range of levels.

The teacher aide will assist the teacher in administering the educational program, particularly the individually prescribed instruction, in areas such as correcting papers, assisting with small group instruction, the administering and scoring of tests, recording data, assisting pupils in getting their materials, the keeping of day-to-day records, and providing feedback information. The intern teacher will perform under the guidance of teachers in the team. In this connection the intern teacher will receive training from the teacher, will help to initiate certain programs, and will also aid the smooth functioning of the overall educational program. The student aides will assist the individual teachers in performing certain duties under the planning and direction of the teaching staff. A detailed outline in the form of a job description is to be prepared delineating functions of teacher aides, student aides and intern teachers.

The building is to be supervised by a curriculum associate who will be in charge of the supervision and implementation of the nongraded philosophy of instruction, and readily available to offer general and specific advice, assistance, guidance and supervision to teachers. However, this is not in any way to be considered a disciplinary position. The curriculum associate will also be responsible for the direct supervision of the individually prescribed instruction. At all times, the curriculum associate will supervise and work with teachers and students, but he will not be responsible for maintaining discipline, nor will he be assigned a teaching load. Therefore, his duties shall include, but not be limited to, the following:

1. Initiating pupil grouping and regrouping in all areas of instruction;

2. Diagnosing through testing to determine students' educational needs;

3. Preparation of weekly master schedule;

4. Guidance of teacher interns;

5. Serving as liaison with administrative, supervisory and supportive personnel as they relate to the team;

6. Assumption of responsibility for reading, mathematics and spelling records;

7. Scheduling field trips and utilizing community and professional personnel to provide enrichment experiences;

8. Scheduling use of space and equipment and conducting general team meetings;

9. Providing supportive guidance to team members in planning and techniques of classroom management;

10. Coordination of audio-visual aids;

11. Planning with special subject teachers, and planning conferences with teachers and parents.

One of the teachers in the team shall serve as team leader. The team leader shall maintain a full teaching assignment and, in addition, assist the curriculum associate in the following areas:

1. Grouping children for instruction in language arts, mathematics, music, art, physical education, social studies, science and health.

2. Assuming a leadership role in team meetings when so designated by the curriculum associate.

3. Preparing the master schedule and guiding teaching interns in their assignments.

4. Coordinating audio-visual aids and initiating assembly programs and related activities in special fields.

5. Planning with special subject teachers in the building.

During the summer, various curriculum committees will be at work devising individual study units in reading, language arts, science, social studies, and other areas to facilitate the complete individualization of instruction.

Although the above arrangements seem to involve a great deal of work to be accomplished in the short period of 180 days, I am confident that if we all work together, as dedicated teams striving for the same goals, we can succeed. In this connection, I WOULD GREATLY APPRECIATE IT IF COMMENTS WITH REGARD TO THE ABOVE PROPOSALS WERE FORTHCOMING FROM ALL TEACHERS.

Please submit your comments and suggestions to your building principal no later than Monday, June 17, 1968.

DISTRICT PRINCIPAL

Appendix F

Wide-Range Attitude Scales
of Behavioral Correlates

A WIDE-RANGE ATTITUDE SCALE OF BEHAVIORAL CORRELATES

PART I

STUDENT'S EVALUATION SCALE ON THE NONGRADED PROGRAM

Recapitulation

Placement

Item	1	2	3	4	5	6	7	8	9	10	11	12	13	14	15	16	17	18	19

Student's Evaluation Scale on the Nongraded Program

Name of Student _____ Age ____ Date of Birth _____
Teacher _____ Date _____

This is not a test. We would like to know how you feel about the nongraded program so that we will know where to make improvements. Check (✓) whether yes or no best expresses your feelings:

	YES	NO
1. Do you feel that the nongraded program does more for you than last year's program?		
2. Do you feel that you get more individual attention in the nongraded program?		
3. Do you work more in a nongraded program?		
4. Has your interest in school increased since being placed in a nongraded program?		
5. Do you think your teacher likes teaching in the nongraded program?		
6. Do your parents like the nongraded program?		
7. Do your classmates like the nongraded program?		
8. Are there any slow students in your class?		
9. Do you like your school?		
10. Have you failed a subject since being placed in the nongraded program?		
11. Do you get poor marks?		
12. Do you feel that you can work by yourself since your placement in the nongraded program?		
13. Are there many more things to learn from the nongraded program?		
14. Do you like the new report card?		
15. Do you like the new parent-student-teacher conferences?		
16. Do you feel that you have learned enough in the nongraded program?		
17. Do your teachers have more discipline problems in a nongraded class?		

	YES	NO
18. Would you like to remain in the nongraded program?		
19. Do you like being placed in a class with other children of several different ages?		

A WIDE-RANGE ATTITUDE SCALE OF BEHAVIORAL CORRELATES

PART II

TEACHER'S EVALUATION SCALE ON THE NONGRADED PROGRAM

Recapitulation

Placement

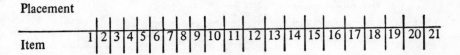

Item

Teacher's Evaluation Scale on the Nongraded Program

Please check (✓) indicating whether yes or no best indicates your feeling about the following:

	YES	NO
1. Do you like being a nongraded teacher?	29	1
2. Do you think that the nongraded program has been effective?	27	3
3. Do you have enough books, supply materials and equipment to individualize instruction?	20	10
4. Do you believe that individual study units have assisted you in individualizing instruction?	30	0
5. Do you prefer multi-age grouping to single age grouping?	25	5
6. Do you feel more contact has been made with the home since you have been a nongraded teacher?	29	1
7. Do you believe that the parents favor the nongraded program?	16	14
8. Do you believe that the students favor the nongraded program?	26	4
9. Can most of your students work independently?	22	8
10. Have most of your students learned how to learn?	21	9
11. Do you like the new report card?	11	19
12. Do you feel that you are more aware of individual differences in students since becoming a nongraded teacher?	25	5
13. Do you believe nongraded education is here to stay?	21	9
14. Have you been able to make better use of your professional skills due to your placement in a nongraded program?	28	2
15. Do you favor team teaching with nongraded education?	30	0
16. Do you believe there should be more nongraded workshops?	25	5

	YES	NO
17. Do you feel that there should be more opportunity for visits to the other nongraded programs?	29	1
18. Do you feel that the entire educational program has improved because of the nongraded program?	29	1
19. Has your students' behavior changed for the better since being placed in a nongraded program?	28	2
20. Is the academic climate more stimulating in a nongraded program?	27	3
21. Do you feel that your fellow teachers favor the nongraded program?	29	1

A WIDE-RANGE ATTITUDE SCALE OF BEHAVIORAL CORRELATES

PART III

PARENT'S SURVEY REGARDING NONGRADED EDUCATION

Recapitulation

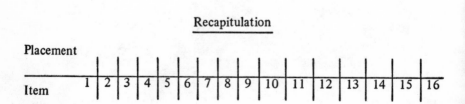

Parent's Survey Regarding Nongraded Education

Name of Parent _____ Date _____

Name of Student _____ Age _____ Date of Birth _____

Your child has been in a nongraded program for approximately one year. We would like to know your attitudes about the nongraded program and how well your child has learned in this new program. Check (✓) whether yes or no best expresses your feelings:

	YES	NO
1. Do you want your child to continue in the nongraded program?	____	
2. Do you believe that your child has learned to work independently?	____	
3. Has your child shown a greater interest in school since being placed in the nongraded program?	____	
4. Do you feel that your child is learning more in the nongraded program than the traditional program?	____	
5. Have your own attitudes about school changed due to the child's placement and performance in a nongraded program?	____	
6. Do you prefer traditional education to nongraded education?	____	
7. Have your interests in the total school program increased?	____	
8. Have your friends and neighbors indicated a preference for the nongraded program?	____	
9. Do you feel that there is more schoolwork for your child to do since his placement in a nongraded program?	____	
10. Do you feel that there is more contact with the home since your child has been placed in a nongraded program?	____	
11. Have you noticed a difference in your child's attitude toward school?	____	

	YES	NO
12. If your answer is yes to number 12, is the difference favorable?		
13. Do you feel that you have received sufficient information about the nongraded program?		
14. Do you feel that the nongraded program has really individualized instruction for your child?		
15. Do you like the new report card?		
16. Do you feel that nongraded education is here to stay?		

Appendix G

Publishers of Programmed Materials

Scholastic
900 Sylvan Ave.
Englewood Cliffs, New Jersey 07632

Encyclopedia Britannica
425 North Michigan Avenue
Chicago, Illinois 60611

Educational Service Inc.
8 Douglas Street
Cortland, New York
Tel: 607-SK.6-2349

SRA Associates
259 East Erie Street
Chicago, Illinois 60611

Kenworthy Educational Services
P. O. 3031
138 Allen Street
Buffalo, New York 14205

Webster Supply Company
Central Warehouse Building
Albany, New York 12207

McGraw-Hill
330 West 42nd Street
New York, N.Y. 10036

Behavioral Research Labs
U.N. Plaza
New York, N. Y.

Harcourt, Brace and World
757 3rd Avenue
New York, N. Y.

Webster Supply Company
Albany, New York

Charles E. Merrill Books Inc.
1300 Alum Creek Drive
Columbus, Ohio 43209

Educational Development Labs
Pulaski Road
Huntington, L.I., New York

Holt, Rinehart Co.
383 Madison Avenue
New York, N.Y. 10017

Science Kit Inc.
Box 69
Tonawanda, N.Y. 14152

Appendix H

Bibliography

Alpren, Morton. *The Subject Curriculum; Grades K - 12.* Columbus: Charles E. Merrill Books, Inc., 1967.

Anderson, Robert A. *Teaching in a World of Change.* New York: Harcourt, Brace & World, Inc., 1966.

Bair, Medill and Richard G. Woodward. *Team Teaching in Action.* Boston: Houghton-Mifflin Company, 1964.

Brown, Frank. *The Appropriate Placement School: A Sophisticated Nongraded Curriculum.* West Nyack, N.Y.: Parker Publishing Company, Inc., 1965.

Brown, Frank. *The Nongraded High School.* Englewood Cliffs, N.J.: Prentice-Hall, Inc., 1963.

Dewey, John. *The School and Society.* Chicago Press, University of Chicago, 1956.

Dufay, Frank R. *Ungrading the Elementary School.* West Nyack, N.Y.: Parker Publishing Company, Inc., 1966.

Durant, William. *Story of Philosophy.* "The Republic, Plato," New York: Simon & Schuster, Inc., 1933.

Goodlad, John I. and Robert H. Anderson. *The Nongraded Elementary School.* New York: Harcourt Brace & World, Inc., 1963.

Hilgard, Ernest R. "Teaching Machines and Creativity," *Stanford Today,* Vol. 1, Autumn, 1963.

McLaughlin, William P. "The Nongraded School - A Critical Assessment," The University of the State of New York, The State Education Department, Associate Director - Research Training Program, September, 1967.

Neagley, Ross L. and N. Dean Evans. *Handbook for Effective Curriculum Development.* Englewood Cliffs, N.J.: Prentice-Hall, Inc., 1967.

Passow, A. Harry. *Education in Depressed Areas.* Teachers College, Columbia University Press, 1963.

Rosenthal, Robert and Lenore Jacobson. *Pygmalion in the Classroom.* New York: Holt, Rinehart, and Winston, Inc., 1968.

Shostak, Arthur B. and William Gomberg. *New Perspectives on Poverty, Educational Reforms and Poverty.* Englewood Cliffs, N.J.: Prentice-Hall, Inc., 1965.

Silberman, Charles E. *Crisis in Black and White.* New York: Random House, Inc., 1964.

Smith, L. L. *A Practical Approach to the Nongraded Elementary School.* West Nyack, N.Y.: Parker Publishing Company, Inc., 1968.

Stagner, Russ and T. F. Korwoski. *Psychology.* New York: McGraw-Hill Book Company, Inc., 1952.

Tewksbury, John L. *Nongrading in the Elementary School.* Columbus: Charles E. Merrill Books, Inc., 1967.

"The Report of the President's National Advisory Commission on Civil Disorders," *New York Times,* New York, N.Y., 1968.

Webster's Seventh New Collegiate Dictionary. Springfield, Mass.: G & C Merriam Co., 1967.

"If it were desired to crush a man completely, to punish him so severely that even the most hardened murderer would quail, it would only be needed to make his work absolutely pointless and absurd. . ."

Dostoevsky

INDEX